WORDS IN PASSING

a selection of formal verse

E.M. SCHORB

ACKNOWLEDGEMENTS

Grateful acknowledgement is given to the following publications in which some of these poems first appeared.

Ascent; The Atlanta Review; Bitterroot; The Blue Unicorn; Candelabrum (UK); The Classical Outlook; College English; The Comstock Review; Cutbank; The Dalhousie Review (CA); The Dark Horse (UK); The Davidson Miscellany, The Deronda Review; Descant; Dream International Quarterly; The Eloquent Atheist; The Fiddlehead (CA); The Formalist; Gallery (UK); The Hampden-Sydney Review; Innisfree Poetry Journal; Insight, Review and Herald Publishing Co.; International Poetry Review; The Journal of Anglo-Scandinavian Poetry (UK); The Journal of New Jersey Poets; Keats Prize Poems, London Literary Editions, Ltd. (UK); Lake Superior Review; Light: A Magazine of Light Verse; The London Poetry Review (UK); Lucid Rhythms; The Lyric; Margie; Measure: A Review of Formal Poetry; Möbius; Noon-Afternoon, American Poetry in Song, Composer, Daniel Jahn; Orbis (UK); Outposts (UK); The Oxford Magazine; Painted Bride Quarterly; Peace is Our Profession: Poems and Passages of War Protest; The Pennsylvania Review; The Phoenix Rising from the Ashes (CA); Plains Poetry Journal; Plainsongs Poetry Magazine; Poet: India; Poet Lore; Poetry Northwest; Poetry Salzburg Review (AT); The Road Not Taken: A Review of Formal Poetry; Roanoke Review; SANE, Inc., Broadside; Shenandoah; The South Carolina Review; The Southern Humanities Review; The Southern Review; The Southern Poetry Review; The Southwest Review; Sparrow; Spring: The Journal of the E.E. Cummings Society; The Texas Review; Thalia (CA); Trinacria; The Unitarian Universalist Magazine; The Wallace Stevens Journal; War, Literature & the Arts: An International Journal of the Humanities (USAF Academy); Wisconsin Review; Writers' Forum; The Yale Review

In Memoriam

Howard Sergeant

Cornel Lengyel

Menke Katz

James Dickey

and for Patricia

CONTENTS

IV. TROUBLE~

V. FORCES~

FOREWARD

What strikes me most about the poems in *Words in Passing*, E.M. Schorb's largest collection to date, containing work from four decades, is their subtle musicality and intellectual range. They demonstrate that Mr Schorb is a poet of great skill and keen wit, a rare formalist whose iambs do not thump and whose ear is attuned to a most intriguing symphony. They hearken back to the great poems of the first half of the twentieth century, to the masterpieces of Robert Frost, John Crowe Ransom, Wallace Stevens, W.H. Auden and William Dickey. They bespeak the presence of a major American poet, one whose mastery of forms is unparalleled and whose voice is resonant, passionate and true long after his book is returned to the shelf.

—Leo Yankevich

I. SOULS ~

O TO BE RICH AND POWERFUL

O to be rich and powerful, to be
like the great-winged dragonfly of the lake,
a jaunty helicopter over sea
whose little motor without spasm spake
of micro- and of macro-cosmic truth;
to say: Littleness is relative, I am
that which I am, younger than in my youth;
imagination's child; a boy like them—
the pirate, prince, or pauper; tree maybe,
no trouble being tree; an open heart;
a mind unmatrixed, ready for the sky
to turn, at will, into the deepest sea;
to put together and to take apart;
rich, powerful to be, and never die!

WORDS IN PASSING

*An apparently homeless occasional visitor to
the Bedford-Stuyvesant Store Front Church,
who signed our Guest Book with an "X," and
was known to our congregants only as the
"shopping cart lady," was crushed by a bus
as she left evening services. Donations
toward her last expenses will be appreciated.*

—*Church Bulletin*

I passed here earlier and saw beneath
a bus an old black woman mocked aloud.
Forty-five minutes saw her ticking, transfixed figure
flouted in blood-filching snow, a crowd's breath
from peace and her God, a corrugated cardboard pyre,
too wet to burn, beneath her Earth-embracing body
and her Earth. Death was an everyday duty,
a boring business, to the busy ambulance
that came too late to save her from her shroud.
And so they chalked this shape of her small fame,
a tableau of her love in white and black,
while the mad mob leaned on linked arms to have
its picture taken by her broken frame.
Here, face down, toward the fiery zodiac,
she saw through Earth and, God please, forgave
that necrophilic crowd, Death's audience.
But in the unseen ceremony of her dying,
before the great beyond of her death, I pray
that they seemed members of her family
and that this reeking street where she was lying
seemed like an avenue of light down which
she went with You and Death without a balk
the while You made her young again and rich;
and that, for Love's sake, You hurried her catafalque,
through traffic-horn salutes and laughter,
beyond her first name, toward her last, and after.

4

MISSIONARIES

Wending our way, we wonder where
the Guys and the Gals went who seem to be gone.
Are we to wander inside of this weather
until we are lost like the others were?

Why were they lost, we wonder moreover,
the brave Moravian men with their women,
the ones in canoes and the cannibals too?
Some seemed to drown in the ever-new river,

some went along for the ride because lonely,
and some never got to the gates made of horn;
but some sought to come back to where they were born,
the ones who cried only, if only, if only.

ELEGY

In Memory of Patrick Harwood-Jones

I

And now the sea is calm, the ebb and flow;
and all the tides of life have come and gone;
and Peace reigns in the mind of my dear friend,
instated like a great calm king, benevolent
and tender, to regard his new domain.

II

My head, an egg, cracked, addled, petrified,
incompetent to solve the cosmic riddle,
in Spring brings forth a Phoenix, but in Fall
twin blackbirds, Time and Death. I write in Fall,
five years from you, in friendship and remembrance.

III

"A man must have his mysteries," you said.
So now, my thoughts upon you, I am blank
to understand, to make some sense of death.
Look! For memento mori I possess
your spectacles, in which I see myself.

IV

Merely the blankest statement, tragic gesture,
as when some friendly hand is flung aloft
above the crowd, remains to keep; a vesper
of evening memory; a prayer I coughed
to save your life that wasn't saved by me.

THE SURVIVOR

The tugs towed us out,   two on each side,
then left us alone.   There loomed the sea,
slate in the slant   of sunlight at dawn;
here, hecatombs hoped,   the hundreds aboard,
boys nearly babies,   boys fat and thin,
homely and handsome,   helmet-haired boys,
among whom myself,   woman-cheeked, pale.
But daylight saw dolphins,   wagging dogs of the sea,
gulls at our garbage   —grand, that display!—
while rainbows rolled butts,   drowned nails of tobacco.
We drilled out on deck,   dodging white wakes,
the escorts escorting   scorned in vainglory.
No sooner sun shined   than set the same sun.
But sharks, shining-finned,   sure found our path.

Not long before light,   a large ship appeared
and held the horizon,   hovering there,
a carrier, cruising,   crossing, recrossing,
then bombers, like bees,   buzzed in the sky.
A bomb amidships!   We scrambled on deck,
where booms lowered boats   as bombs blew them up.
No escorts escaped!   Scrapped in the deep!
Our shuddering ship,   shadowed with death,
slid on its side   and sank slowly down.
I rose on a raft   and reached for survivors.
Hope in my hand,   I hauled them aboard:
boys nearly babies,   boys fat and thin,
homely and handsome,   helmet-haired boys,
among whom myself,   woman-cheeked, pale.

MADAM'S HOUSE, 1913, A SUITE

A House is not a home.
—Polly Adler

1. TIPPY'S SONG ON A RAINY DAY

Once Madam told, sipping champagne,
how poverty built her disgrace.
What is the loss? What is the gain?
Poor Madam wears silk hose and lace
while her smug family reside
in Potter's Field's lowly embrace—
all things will level with the tide.

My Johnny feared the ball-and-chain
and left me flat, a welfare case.
What is the loss? What is the gain?
These days I love at a faster pace
than any ordinary bride!
Though Johnny's gone and left no trace,
all things will level with the tide.

When I was good, they called me plain.
The simple farmboys would grimace.
What is the loss? What is the gain?
Now men come to this sultry place
and, smiling, up to me they stride.
It seems that sin improves my face.
All things will level with the tide.

On rainy days I watch the rain
that falls straight down like tears outside.
What is the loss? What is the gain?
All things will level with the tide.

2. LOVE'S ILLUSIONS

The naked truth will lie.
I don't believe in facts.
What's in the inner eye
Is what the outer lacks.

We see just what we wish,
No matter near or far.
Plain talk is gibberish.
The moon's a scimitar.

The night's an Arab's sheet
Of swirling blue and black.
The Earth is at his feet,
The stars are at his back.

And even love is true
If we should make it so.
Oh lover, love me too!
Oh lover, let me go!

3. TIPPY REMEMBERS LAWYER SMYTHE

"The men I fancy most,
they have erectile heads
like the cobra-di-capello.
You remember what they tell O
of the pleader, now a ghost,
how the veins of his neck would swell O
and his face in different reds
would flush until the flesh
stretched like a taut balloon?
Expansion of his meaning,
like an increasing wish,
was forced by the poor fellow
to the point of apoplexy.

We girls could only swoon.
For oh, his paroxysms,
how eloquent they were,
as if he were unspleening
himself of his hauteur
(we called him Mister Sexy,
but just among ourselves:
it was one of our witticisms,
or better, barbarisms;
because he wasn't like that at all).
I smile to think about him,
and yet it casts a pall
(it's sad when memory delves
like a baited hook on a line
and suddenly has a weight).
What shall we do without him,
we who loved him well O?
What shall we do without him,
that bulbous-headed fellow?"

4. CAPITULATION

Be near me now; Time's weakened me; be
near me now; let me have my way once more.
Forgive, forget; you must remember me
now in my need. Come in the door,
sit down, relax, and let us talk
of all the silence listened for
these many years. I walk
alone in here and putter
weakly. I'm white as chalk.
Perhaps, I mutter,
in truth, it's I,
who could not utter
a cry,
must sigh . . . .

5. THE BROKEN CROW

Along the cliffs she wandered,
    a song sublimely sung,
along the cliffs, and pondered
    the sea they overhung—

"The sea is vast and deep,
    the cliffs are high and wide.
Now let me plunge in sleep,
    and in black water hide

my body that is dying
    away from loving friends,
away from any crying
    and have the best of ends."

It was a swan who dove
    into the sea below:
next day at Fisher's Cove
    they found a broken crow.

Her friends were there and crying.
    It was the worst of ends.
Oh, she who had been dying
    could never make amends.

A CONUNDRUM

The child knows little but "I am the future,"
  and only knows this as a vague surmise.
  What comes too slowly ever to surprise
soon grows as fact into a fuller picture,
producing for all children a first stricture,
  the grip of life. So soon they realize
  how limited is life's sweet new-won prize,
how can they know their nature from their nurture?

  How can we know just who we are at heart,
when what surrounds us is an imperative
  which sets us off in a small world apart
from that in which all others try to live?
  I wish the world were open from the start,
so we could have our truest hearts to give.

LATE SLEEPER

She never woke without the smile
that shaped that rose, her pretty mouth.
She'd lift the telephone and dial
for breakfast; then she'd have her bath,
cheerfully free from righteous wrath.

There was no need to wait a while
to travel, study, learn a style:
her money made her polymath.
    She never woke.

After her bath she'd ride a mile
around the park, in single file,
with other girls of luck and wealth,
for poise, and skill, and better health,
and wonder what one *could* revile.
    She never woke.

DESCANT

O Meister, liebster Meister mein!
—Goethe

His American granddaughter, the nurse, called him Pops.
When she came home from work, she needed *Schnapps*.
Ich weiss nicht, weiss nicht. . . Aber der Herr
Tod lebt. Vielleicht ist er an der Tür.

Away in his own room she could hear Pops sing
a broken, depressing *Lied*—his own thing.
Herein, Herr Tod! Ich bin allein,
"O Meister, liebster Meister mein!"

Her grandmother gave her chocolate for her tears.
She knew Pops missed his *Liebchen*—married fifty years!
Ich weiss nicht, weiss nicht. . . Obgleich
diese Schwärze ist irgendwie lehrreich.

Why did her hard old Pops sit alone in the dark?
She nursed old people now—took Pops to the park.
Mein Haar ist grau, meine Backen sind blau.
Nun ich muss schlafen, mit meinem Blut lau.

She was middle-aged herself, a white-smocked Valkyrie,
but still a little girl underneath a tree.
Bis morgen, Herr Tod! Ich bin müde und alt.
Wie die Bäume im Winter, ich bin sehr kalt!

She'd be off to the old in the nursing home tomorrow,
to face again the selfsame sadness, the selfsame sorrow.
Man kann, was man will, wenn man nur will, was man kann.
We can do what we will, if we *will* to do what we can.

DETECTIVE STORY

Came in two hip nuns in unnunlike "funny"
disguise, and he who had been standing there,
sipping a pop, showed such interest—he
eyed them with eyes gone cold, studied what they were
in such strange dark habit and ivory-
embroidered cloaks—and so wondered, wondered

so plainly, as if he wanted them to know,
that they felt him there and turned toward
him, looking him over, eyeing him now,
wondering who this turkey was, some young cop,
some dude; but then, with bows, turned back to
order to-go burgers, containered pop,

straws sticking from eyed lids, and pulled rolls of bills
to pay with, flashing them; and, heeled, tapped
into the street, calling back, "You want girls?
Come on, then, boy!" Guffaws. And he followed them.
He kept his distance, though—for "speed kills"—
like a real cop, tailing them, shepherding lambs

to slaughter; for ahead there, in shadow, at
the far end of the street, waited Sam,
his partner. He'd signal Sam, by tipped hat,
to take the tail up soon, and he would drop back
to see what else was "going down," root
out some more crime, and then take in a flick.

KWAME AND DUTCH
Note: In Africa, AIDS is often
referred to as the thin disease.

We worked on the New York docks,
off-loading ships, on-loading trucks.
Sick and a former junkie, Kwame shirked.
He bled from the rectum when he worked.
The bleeding reached such an intensity,
we had to rush him to the Emergency.
Later, the surgeons cut the grapes away.
Released, he hobbled to a bar nearby
as if he walked on broken glass,
a knot of stitches in his new tight ass.

He put a long-boned arm over my shoulder
in the manner of someone wiser, older,
and wheezed, "Dutch, I'm going to die.
The blood tests say that I
've got the thin disease."
He gave my shoulder a squeeze.
"I got it from being heedless
about the stinking dirty needles."

And soon, he took sick. The white bed
was empty but for Kwame's wave-crested,
black skull, and the clear, draining hoses.
Next to his bed was a jar of posies
one of his girlfriends had brought.
Now Ghana was a faraway thought,
but I was there, with him, near.

He could see me clearly
if he looked, holding his bony hand
that wore an African wedding band—
and I am there now, again, as he lingers,
our funny different-colored fingers
entwined, though pulling apart,
breaking my hard Dutch heart.

16

AN EVENING WITH "BLOOD"

Art, being bartender, is never drunk;
And magic that believes itself, must die. . .
                              —Peter Viereck

Just call when you hit town, the great man wrote.
I like your work, and we must talk about it.
We lived a state apart, an hour's drive,
and I had business there. I called him up,
and he invited us to "Come right out,"
to hurry to his house, "and help me drink
a quart of Southern Comfort that a student
of mine has given me—I need some help.
Today above all days I need some help—
a falling down, and then a falling out!
How soon?" he asked. "As soon as we can get there."
We didn't even have to ring the bell.
The bard swayed hugely at his door to greet us.
"I've got *your* names locked in. You call me Blood.
It was my nickname when I was a kid.
I like your husband's work," he told my wife.
"It's very individual—which I,
and Emerson, and Wallace Stevens, think
is most important. Possum doesn't, though,
but he is wrong." The lakeside house was empty
but for the three of us, a huge TV—
the N.F.L. in combat filled the screen—
and roaring fans and players, who loomed large.
"It's an old game. I like to run the plays
and second guess with twenty-twenty hindsight.
I tore your poems apart like that and found
I couldn't take much out—that's good!
Don't write, re-write! I drop them and go back.
This took five years—to make a wall of words
stand up like that. I worked spasmodically.
The novel took ten years, but it was worth it.
It brought a lot of money, and the movie,

17

and the chance for me to play a part myself.
That's Blood up on the screen, that character.
He'd scare the shit out of you, wouldn't he?
That wasn't acting, that was really me.
You see this arrow? Penetrate skull-bone.
Know how to use a crossbow? Here, I'll show you.
Up—like that—that's right. Now you aim and fire.
Bring down a rhino, that thing would. But Blood
says that you need another drink, and then
I'll play the banjo for you. Read me this one—
the one about the mad marine. I *love* it,"
he told my wife. "I love the really mad ones.
Did you see how I got myself arrested?
Drunk driving. What I do is brownbag out
into the woods and turn my highbeams on
and try to see above them, not the helmet
of ordinary life down here. You too?
We yearn for levitation, flights of fancy.
I flew a lot of missions in the war.
Yes, Blood has done a major share of burning,
incendiaried towns and populations,
and no one ever understands you right
again when you've done that. My explanation
is in my poetry for those with guts to know.
As for the rest, I cannot help the world.
Above the high beams is the zodiac.
Let fools ask there about this fire-bombed world.
Blood's in the dark—like him—like you, sweet lady."

TO MENKE KATZ

O
Menke,
with your sweet
mandolin and
thick-accented song,
your poetry of
burning villages and
brave forays beyond the pale,
of coming to America
and golden Lower East Side streets,
of the secret laughter at the center
of the most Holy Kabbalah, O Menke,
for you, dead at nearly ninety, I write
this Katzian sonnet. The body sleeps to free the soul.

NORMA JEAN

I was a student then and waited in
the office of a famous acting coach,
and in came Marilyn Monroe. I grinned,
but she was self-involved, not to approach.
It had begun to rain, the window showed,
and she showed too, rain on her London Fog,
blue scarf, pulled tight below her chin and bowed,
rain running down her face. I was agog,
but tried my best not to disturb her, not
to make my presence felt. She looked afraid,
and pale, and wet, and small, and sad. She seemed
so regular a pretty girl that I forgot
she was a movie star and saw instead
a girl from home of whom I'd always dreamed.

PARIS RECIDIVIST

The sea-tax brought us down: my state,
after all, was operating a protection
racket, as you Chicagoans might call it.
It was a dirty game, but there you are,
it was the only game in town.
Located as we were over the mouth of
the Hellespont, we controlled all traffic
going east. For a while, everybody paid,
and we got on quite well. Troy was small,
even by the standards of the age: she had
nothing to sell—oh, nothing worth
considering—but she had the trade route,
had it by its watery throat, and everybody knew
and didn't seem to mind. Of course,
there's always something building,
but our hold was strong. No tax,
no trading with the East. It all seemed
fair enough and, somehow, to the others,
a natural thing. Then I did it,
gave the Greeks exactly what they needed:
an excuse. Helen, poor Helen, she gloried
in one thought: that it was she,
and not the sea, for whom we fought.

WALLACE STEVENS CONTEMPLATES SUNDAY SERVICE IN HADDAM

The day was nooning toward its bells,
and all were late, and yet he lingered there

enjoying summer and gold-nugget bees
divorced from gravity. He felt, at last,

that he was master of his mind, one of
the few who've made a satisfying picture

of the world and of the world's world,
the inclusive all, the one containing

all the perfect particles, the one
he was among the ones of, watching as

his hand scooped air as if it were
ice cream, a clean fresh strawberry,

an air so clean it glittered to his eyes
and melted on his tongue, an air

of summer on a Sunday. He wouldn't go,
and finally the others left him there.

NEAR CHRISTMAS

I

Now in November winter is half turning
on autumn down the land from Maine to Jersey,
and Christians think of Christmas. Bargain basements
hum with the hymns of shoppers who are yearning
for the millennium of peace; but hearsay
has it that trouble brews. The icy casements
of early winter, frigid films of frost,
portend now, and remind the multitude
of Christmas shoppers to count up the cost
of (being human) being bad or good.

II

In all the avenues and cross streets of
Manhattan Island, how the atmosphere
improves! One notices an unexpected
smile, kindness; odd euphoria of love
pervades the frigid evening air; the fear
of strangers is diminished; unaffected
good humor rises, rampant; Noel! Noel!
sounds in, or seems to sound in, every voice.
Now only Heaven's true; there is no Hell!
This is the season to forgive, rejoice!

A YELLOW CROSS

It's sad to write this on Memorial Day,
a sonnet on the subject of a draft
that's over now, but hasn't gone away,
like writing of a bribe, or ugly graft,
upon a day we honor something great,
like life these dead have given for our sake,
like courage in the face of awful threat,
like freedom we must make and then remake.

But being vet and patriotic codger,
I am compelled to write of one Unknown
whose grave is empty of its own draftdodger,
containing as it does no skeleton—
the green mound topped with a low yellow cross
as if ashamed to represent no loss.

LETTERS HOME

(An R.A.F. Pilot, Bermudan, Age 21; 1943)

I am on standby at flights,
or flying from ten until ten.
That's from the A.M. to A.M.

I return in the morning and sleep
until tea-time, get up and have tea,
and then see a cinema show.

After the flicks I walk back,
go to mess, and to bed about ten.
So at long last I'm on operations.

I enclose the newspaper clipping
to show you my handiwork.
I got the two hits dead amidships.

God, I was thrilled! But don't think
that I gloat on the enemy dead—
just glad that I wasn't afraid.

The Maltese are marvelous people,
always so cheerful and smiling.
They really deserve the George Cross.

The hotel at which I am billeted
is situated on the sea front
at Sliema, so when I wake mornings

I can look out my window and see
the white Mediteranean waves
on water as blue as Bermuda's.

Over sea, out of Tunis, past Sicily,
off Naples, their Wellington fell.

They took to their rubber dinghy

and had drifted for thirty-nine hours
when the Italians reported them down.
The Germans, at last, picked them up.

(A FELLOW PRISONER TO THE PILOT'S MOTHER)

Madam, any attempt at escape
is infused with a great deal of danger,
the success of it usually being

more a matter of luck than design.
It so happened that I had myself
been preparing to make an attempt

when he came to me late on the eve
of his transfer by train from the camp.
I did not have the chance that he did,

so it seemed like the right thing to do
to surrender my maps and my compass
and whatever provisions I had.

His journey commenced in the morning.
When it showed itself likely to end
before darkness could cover his flight,

he decided to make his escape
in the full light of day, at first chance.
Now to jump from a train in the dark

is an orthodox mode of escape,
but to make such a break in broad day
involved so much greater a risk.

But your Jimmy accepted that risk.
As his train was held up in a station

26

he was able to knock out his guard

and to leap out and run down the platform.
But the guards in the other compartments
saw, and repeatedly fired.

(A British Nurse to the Pilot's Mother)

The cemetery is outside the town,
so was saved from the worst battle scars.
When I found it this morning, my dear,

your young Jimmy's sad grave was at peace
and had flowers, carnations and roses,
which were left there by persons unknown.

The Italians erected a stone
with his name and the date of his death
and the fact of his being a pilot,

but unfortunately this was toppled
by some bombs which had landed nearby.
Two young Tommies were visiting graves

and they helped me to prop the stone up,
and we took several photos beside it
which I'll forward as soon as developed.

Now the padre has promised to make
a large white wooden cross
and to put on it "Outerbridge, James,"

and the crest of the R.A.F.
and that he was born in Bermuda.
He isn't alone among strangers.

There are Yanks and Canadians, too.
It's a beautiful spot, with the sea,

like the sea of Bermuda, in sight.

(FROM HIS LAST LETTER)

. . . My Rhodes at Oxford is waiting,
so I study my Latin and Greek.
American sports are the thing,

and I play at softball every day
and am keeping quite physically fit.
You can learn almost anything here,

from chess to trombone playing,
and my program is so well arranged
that I haven't a moment to spare. . . .

*But this last letter wasn't received
until more than a year after he
had been killed. It had obviously*

*travelled through many countries,
for it bore seven censorship stamps,
including the swastika.*

THE WEEPING BUTCHER

for Jack Parker, R.I.P.

The butcher weeps for onions, not for steak,
and yet he is capable of heartache.

One day he came out smiling
from the refrigerator—"You *are* beguiling."

The lady tittered—"A sweet man, Smith."
He ground her up some chuck forthwith.

But why do you drink, butcher, hiding in back?
When you have wife, children, home, what do you lack?

Smiling, pig's head in hand, he shrugs.
Blood's on his apron. The pig's head winks and mugs.

Poet, butchers aren't so different from us,
only they don't make such a fuss.

ATGET

Great Atget took his time.
A picture was no chance,
unlike a lucky rhyme
unknown in advance.

Patiently, he stood
waiting for the light.
His camera wore a hood.
The sun must come up right.

And now his photographs
show us Paris then.
And no one these days laughs
at such patient men

as pioneered the picture
so that painters paint
no more a literature
proving memory faint,

but finally engage
with true imagination,
while on every page
he shows La Belle, his nation.

MISS LONELY HEARTS

"Love wearies me as water wearies stone.
Love baffles me as time must baffle clocks.
Love gnaws at me as dogs gnaw at a bone.
Love makes me feel as if I've eaten rocks."
You love someone because you have no choice.
You like someone but not someone you love.
You love someone but not someone you like.
You need to hear that one and only voice.
"Let's top the sea-cliff on a roaring bike.
Let's be in blue, together. Let love go!
Let's leap for water from that place above.
Let's watch and see death happening below."
I feel your pain, no need for explanation.
I understand your hopeless situation.

BOWERY BLUES

O, it's sick green walls
   with a painted comet
and checkerboard tiles
   inlaid with vomit—
oh, if God made a fool
   you can bet I'm it,
old lady on the bum!

O, it's "Cover your cough!"
   on a cardboard sign,
and it's "def no credit"—
   ah, what a line
for a biddy whose blood
   is ninety per wine,
old lady on the bum!

O, its "The Big Boy Shot,"
   that's the morning double:
for thirty-five cents
   it'll cure my trouble.
I sit down next
   to a tramp with a stubble—
old lady on the bum!

O, it's the Salvation Army
   when I need a bed,
or I just take my shoes
   and put 'em under my head
and lie in a doorway
   and wish I was dead—
old lady on the bum!

O, I'll die someday
    of this rotgut booze,
but what do I care?
    I got nothing to loose.
I loose all I have
    when I loose my blues!
Old lady on the bum!

THE GOOD ONES

for Elbert Harkins

I guess the good ones stay with everyone,
   the ones we knew who made us proud to know
them at some point somewhere beneath the sun,
   but, to the good, I think, the others go
into a fading place and so are lost,
   the others who were not so good to know.
The pain of course stays like an ugly ghost.
   But I suppose in time it too will go.
I could name names, but only of the good,
   the ones I knew that I was proud to know.
They are the heros of my life. I would
   keep them forever fresh, not let them go.
It isn't hard to keep the two apart,
the heros and the zeros of the heart.

ART

His lens held a sea like rocks
from the side of a tossing vessel.
But the film couldn't see the colors
for the movement of up and down,
and clouds that shut out the sun,
in the snap of the snarling sea,

and left him a picture of rocks,
a film of hard-labor cut out
of a field of hammered stone,
and paint that had bled and blended.
He lost his way in the image
he held enlarged before him,

a rocklike Pollock of greens,
of blues and even of reds,
not a sea- but a lunar landscape,
not a lunar but Martian, maybe,
where convicts had worked in a swelter
and dropped in their tracks one day.

Now, looking flat at the thing,
hanging walled as a square on brown,
it tilted strangely away,
into the brown of the wall,
and no further angling would work.
What troubled him was that he saw,

clearly, in its strange unclearness,
the graph of a feckless life,
and terrain of the place where it lived,
his art in a criminal pile
of a hybrid of land and sea,
and the day of his germ in chaos,

35

spinning wildly forward in time
from where it must always have come,
some dimension of a kind unknown
to the rational light of day,
and he let the print fall from the wall
and slide at his feet on the floor.

And he walked there, on that sea
of carven and sharpened stone,
on that rocky path, where water
had frozen into strange land.
He would walk there, gone from this world,
till he found what it was he had lost.

THE ORPHANED

When the mood comes upon him to die
of a loneliness deeper than death,

he must speak to himself like a parent
in a lecturing voice, but with love.

He must be his own father and mother,
and at night when he looks up at heaven,

where nothing of earth seems to live,
and the range of all things is so great

as to startle the love from his breast,
he must think of his father, the Rock,

and of his mother, the Dead Sea, and of
the message he brings from the sun.

MILK

The child wakens to the first snow,
(noted), of its lifetime, and says: "Milk."
The mother takes it out so it can know
that snow is frozen water, slippery as silk,
paler than vanilla in a cone, harder, softer,
the strangest thing on Earth, so far,
stranger than its yellow urine. The mother
tugs it through the drifts, into the car,
straps it in, shakes her head like a puppydog,
and sprinkles baby's cheeks. Baby giggles.
Window-wipers make pretty window-fans. The rug
across its lap is hot and baby wiggles
to be free of it. They seem to climb the sky.
Everywhere they look the white stuff
is. It takes them to a cloud that has an eye
of darkness, surrounded by pale puff.
But it's the supermarket sign. Mother
takes excited baby in and buys some things.
Some day, she says, you'll have a little brother.
Baby doesn't understand, so sings:
caroo, caroo, milk, milk, milk. . . Baby thinks:
it's fun and frightening, too. Curled
up, back in the car, baby, dreaming, drinks
the whole white gallon of the world.

MARKED MAN

He looks for Death
back over his shoulder,
some say too much.

He looks for Death
ahead on the hill there,
perhaps an inch.

ONCOMING COMPANY

Oncoming company:
the flooding tides, the fell
ingrowing grave, the sea
of place, the held in hell.
What dark, what bleak o'clock
swings pendulously now?
No record on a rock
survives the voice and vow.

No record on a rock
survives the voice and vow:
Swings pendulously now
that dark, that bleak o'clock
of place, the held in hell
ingrowing grave, the sea
of flooding tides, the fell
oncoming company.

HADEWIJCH IN WALL STREET

When I walk in our ancient millioned alley
and dream of my Dutch past, I find my father,
a fortune-hunting youth who could not know
that flannel suits and frilly office frocks
are gray or parti-colored walking shrouds.

What terrible ecstasy would you have brought
this padded bourgeoisie, mad Hadewijch,
Dutch poet-nun who'd copulate with God?

The need for exaltation that I feel
in morbid secret service to my soul,
I walk like a mad soldier on patrol
among my enemies, the dressed to kill.

OBITUARY
Edwin Marsh Schorb, Sr. (1893-1963)

> *Success is counted sweetest*
> *By those who ne'er succeed.*
> *—Emily Dickinson*

Without the mummeries of death, by fire,
but not by burning but by breath of smoke,
you died like some high god upon his pyre:
O quick, barbaric, merciful good luck!

I had so many fears for you, my father;
your ribald binges must have racked your body;
I feared some lingering illness, and I'd rather
have anything attacking one so bawdy

than an unthrilling, invalided life
spent somehow to its end in spite and temper;
though there was one thing sterner than its strife:
no death, no anything could make you whimper!

Your life was preparation for its pain:
you trained for ill and not for good, as Housman
advised his blear-eyed Shropshire lad to train
when, "moping melancholy mad," that yeoman

had rhymed the cow to death. A country boy
yourself, of Dutch and Anglo-Saxon stock,
New Jersey born and bred, hobbledehoy
and shining-faced, at fourteen, to New York

you went, in Nineteen-Hundred-Seven, to be
a runner on the New York Stock Exchange:
No more a rube!—No more a nonentity!—
but now (or then) a Wall Street runner, plung-

ing through the frantic, money-making crowds

41

America's romantic myth had brought
to conquer fortunes (time, events, becloud
so far-bygone an era, the magic sort

of moment that it was, the innocence
of fledgling fortune-hunters like yourself,
whose world of thought was Yankee common sense
and industry, who dreamed a sweet success

sometimes into existence in a trice:
opposing Mogul, Robber-baron, Tycoon,
all those first-comers who had set the price
of your success so high, O youngest son!)

Your struggle was a long one: studying
beside a late oil-lamp, O handsome youth
with raven hair!—your eyes only seeing
great dreams—reading of Rome, in law—in faith

that "Education makes the man;" with knowledge,
as Bacon'd put it, being power. Your roommate,
a brilliant graduate of Harvard College,
who one day would become a diplomat,

and later on Ambassador-at-large
in a long dead administration, instructed
you in "polish," as if you were his charge:
"Marry a rich woman," he told you once, "Ed.

That's my advice to you. I mean to do it
myself." Indeed, that's what he did. Not you,
though. Women meant too much. They knew you
  knew it,
too, handsome twenty-one, bonds salesman now,

and "Coming," as they called it then; they knew,
and loved you for it; helped you to establish
your reputation on The Street, and strew
themselves like flowers at your feet, flashing

their smiles like diamonds, their gems like teeth,
attracting and repelling, always rich
and husbanded by ghosts—a jewelled wreath
of Marley'd widows, beauties, and rich bitches,

young and old, fell about your frail young shoulders
—the day was almost won for Trumpery!
But meanwhile now the world was hurling boulders
of War, had been since Ferdinand, Humpty-Dumpty

of Peace, had fallen from the caving wall
at Sarajevo, four trenched and bloody years
before—time now for you to heed the call!
You went with other would-be "Officers

and Gentlemen" to be inducted, and
trained in the arts of martial leadership;
but suddenly, amazingly, they hand-
ed you your discharge.—We had won, had whipped

King Billy and the Ottoman Empire
(for better or for worse the deed was done!)
—and you, handsome young E.M. Schorb, Esq.,
were free to enter stormy Prohibition,

that time of Ought-not, But, and All-be-damned,
when "bathtub was synonymous with gin;"
an Eighty-nine-day-wonder, you had lammed
back into mufti—lost the veteran's pension

for my dear mother's Merry Widowhood;
but not your fault—a bureaucratic trick
that politicians played on Motherhood
is what we'll call it, for a sad laugh's sake.

Your first wife was a dopefiend. She's long dead.
The next an upright nurse—good family;
tubercular, although Bermuda bred;

and oh, British to the bone; unamatory,

or so you said, although you got a son
by her;—but not in Colorado, where
you went to help her lungs, and met someone
more amatory—Governor's daughter

she was: young, bright, and burning in her britches:
Black-Bottoming and Charlestoning and being
filled with a Flapper's ripe and bitching itches
—until you ran away from both of them.

By now you'd made the magic book—*WHO'S WHO*.
Success had come. You worked out of New York
and lived "Uptown"—and then the Market threw
its curve: Black Tuesday, Twenty-nine. What work

of evil genius had occurred? O fell
green hand of money! Lost hey-days! Your wife
was gone! Your son was gone, taken. What Hell
had happened and had happened here? What grief?

When, still young, you rode the Elevated,
the rumble of the wheels ground down your heart:
that iron-roar made you think quick death was fated,
thuswise against ambition raised your guard.

From then on you'd inveigh against that world
of Business, Finance, Property, Possessions
that you were trained in. Overboard you hurled
it, calling afterwards impedimenta

whatever slightest trinket stuck to you
as to summer-melting wax, which washed away
itself,—before the pierce-eyed public view!—
whatever'd stuck. The haberdashery

was all you kept: the custom-tailored suit;
silk tie; the Homburg hat; the shining shoes:

44

as you had worn them through the Prohibition Toot
you wore them through the sad Depression Days;

the Fylfot-War; the Eisenhower Fifties. . .
when I was there to know you, aging father:—
I, growing up by then, you in your sixties,
hair briny with the years, a heavy breather,

but still a regal, leucomelanous head—
bared now ("The man who never wears a hat"
was what they called you then—you were ahead
of time, before the style, an old pace-set-

ter—Kennedy would make bare heads official
—"My reason is to save my head of hair;
hats stop the circulation," you said; "this'll
become the style, when people learn.") Never

will I forget those idiosyncratic
quirks, those oddnesses, that set you apart
from ordinary beings so dramatic-
ally! I, walking by your side in Newark,—

where we then lived, deep in a basement flat,
where roaches climbed the walls like living paper,
and damp night brought the rustle of a rat,
—would glow to see the people look, O happier

than a rich son, to be the son of one
so striking and distinguished in appearance!
"That gent I seed you wid, are you his son?"—
yet of the poor we were among the poorest!

You'd married Mom in Nineteen-Thirty-Two,—
one year before Repeal, deep in Depression
days. Having met in a speakeasy, you
decided to continue partying—

and did throughout the years, by fits and starts!

45

Though making money was a difficulty
that interfered with freedom, your free hearts
went on their merry way, higgledy-piggledy,

from the Honeymoon Hotel, here in New York,
where you escaped the bill by wearing all
your wardrobe out the door, until the stork
dropped in your lap a wet, if "Wonderful!"

responsibility—which you were not
quite ready to live up to, though you tried—
"To be father, now! Why, I've forgot-
ten how to burp a child! I'm forty-five!"

Soon fifty-five! Now, door-to-door, you sold:
bandaids, thread, pots and pans, encyclopedias
(once more you carried Bacon's quote in bold
lettering on a business card, *KNOWLEDGE*

IS POWER!)—Oh, a library of books!
Ah, melancholy-morbid! How you read
"The Raven," with your Barrymorish looks
to help you dramatize as you recited!

And "To the Ladies!" How that angered Mom!
You made her Judy O'Grady, not the Lady,
while you remained the Colonel! Deaf and dumb
with anger, she would wait until payday

before she made things up. The years went by.
You went to work at managing hotels
for some cheap chain; then later you would try
your hand at selling real estate; but selling

was too rough now, Old Charmer, sixty-five!
And then you read De Quincey and De Ropp:
"Why, I have never even been alive!"
And that was how you found your way to dope!

To dope and death as well! For you left home,
went to a hobo rooming house downtown,
and, three weeks later—dead! O poor poor Mom!
"I loved him. Understood him? No." She frowned.

SIX DEAD IN BLAZE IN NEWARK, the paper said:
I read the headlines on the Hudson Tube
while on my way to Newark. Could you be dead?
Yes, I identified you at the Morgue!

Without the mummeries of death, by fire,
but not by burning but by breath of smoke,
you died like some high god upon his pyre:
O quick, barbaric, merciful good luck!

THE POOR BOY

Not having had inheritance or luck,
undemocratically good blood or breeding,
nor any gold come out of family stock
that sets a young man up, preceding
maturity and forming for it pride
in action and aristocratic strength,
solace in having purpose in each stride,
and discipline that carries to its length,
I've found myself romantically inclined,
a muzzy mongrel with a barking mind.

How I admire those men and women who
were reared in order, dignity and pride!
You see it in their eyes, a voiceless vow,
a knowledge Levelling denied.
Here now is social change preeminent,
the mass man rises to his rightful place;
but his ascension leaves a remanent
of unredeemable darkness of disgrace
in that all art must kowtow to a taste,
now at his rising, weaned on gutter waste.

I know, for I have foraged in the lots
of blackened cities looking for a prize
of red discarded unbroken flowerpots
to place my plants, to brighten eyes.
I've shined a thousand shoes along the streets
of coughing cities all across this land.
A child, I'd enter taverns and retreats
the like of which to others would be banned.
Oh, I know poverty, unhappiness;
such things I know, I have no need to guess.

And yet a sturdy strength comes out of it,
that's undeniable; but at what cost!
The strength of street-bred children is their wit
and nerve; nobility is lost

in the hungry race of mongrels for a bone,
and Honor hangs his head before the scene.
The heart of the street urchin is a stone
ground more with each engagement, until mean.
We learn to fight and hate, but not to love,
no matter who says so. We learn to shove.

WILDWOOD

I have few memories of a happy childhood,
but spells of happiness, short spells, occurred.
Sometimes I was happy out in Wildwood,
which echoed with the whisper of the Word.

To run and play on grass as green as can be,
who all-eyes had the city streets to play,
was for a child a visit full of candy,
a Christmas on a humid summer day.

ANTHOLOGIES ARE SAD

Impressed by smoking-ember music,
as I have always been, drinking gin,
and reading the poets of the past—
who are in anachronistic pain
as if alive, striving, thriving
today—I think of today's.

I have a new anthology,
one including me,
with, alas, dates.
Most have only births and dashes,
a few the flying ashes,
the smoking music, of the past—
dates that say, *At last! At last!*

What then of Berryman
and those other merry men
and women who were human—
in pain and joy—alive?
In the anthologies they thrive,
possessing their due dates!

So now I turn a page,
afraid to find my final age;
and, though my last is but a dash,
I feel the flutter of ash.

II. LOVE ~

A TUMBLE FOR SKELTON

Wherein Margaret Patricia Hill is Championed

Well done,
sweet John!
But I'd make a bet
that my Margaret
could contest against
that *midsummer flower*
that *hawk of the tower*
whom you have advanced,
in summer assaulting,
in tumbling in down,
who would be vaulting
but never be faulting
but always be salting
sweet red tomatoes
and spreading her toes
and sticking her breasty
where Philip was roosting
and cooing for fair
out of that lair
into the air
where her heart would be pounding
and pulses resounding
to the tapping of toes
in little high heels
of glittering shoes,
not spinning her wheels,
charming John,
you old Don Juan.

Yes, I'd take the bet
that my Margaret
ungauded, ungirdled,
in a contest had hurtled
beyond your yon Hussey

like a beautiful horsey
or a flying flamingo
and be all ago
so joyously
so womanly
her demeaning
in everything
far far passing
that I can indite
or suffice to write
how superiorly
my lady would be
to Margaret Hussey
to make her seem fussy
and in the end dusty
and yet even musty
and leave her behind
never to find
while my winning lady
would take prize
at flashing her eyes
on that gay day
and laurel for her head
and goose feathers in bed,
but your lady, dear John,
you sweet old Don Juan,
your lady'd be lead
compared with my Margaret,
and I'd make that bet!

THE REQUEST

In her grave smile, I saw
myself reflected, too,
in a likeness not too near,
not as some unified law,
but as one whom I knew
before her face was there,
one from inside of me,
so whom I could not see.

And I reached out to her
across a deepening flood,
and asked if she could see
in my bleak-featured stare
and dark, unrisible blood,
her own grave self in me,
and if she could, advise
death be not recognized.

LOVE STORY

In no time at all
love had us fall
headlong.
My doubtful heart
had kept us apart
too long.

Then, suddenly,
I learned to see
and trust
you whom I held
for your eyes willed
my trust.

Now, holding your hand,
I understand
your touch—
the palm's gentle shove
of my heart toward love—
I'm rich!

WANT OF TIME

Two weeks were plenty in those days
before we met for words of praise,
but now two weeks are not enough
to express to you my degree of love.
For in those days I knew no one
who could undo words as they were done
by gaining beauty and new light
much faster, love, than I can write.

But now, my dear, while charged with love,
I have this failing, seen above:
I can't design around your hair
accomplished words, express and fair,
for it improves at such a rate
it leaves me in a wordless state.
Nor can I write a faint disguise
with speed enough to cloak your eyes.

Ah, no, my love, it's of no use
to match my words, to their abuse,
against improving loveliness
and leave the words to mean the less!
I'll not do harm to poetry
trying to say what I can see.
Instead, I'll simply say that I
will follow through Eternity
until your beauty's all around
and I am left within, quite sound,
to sing that anniversary—
Millenium of You and Me!

BUCOLIC SONG

When dead dreams are dreamt anew
  as my once dead ones are,
homage must be paid to you,
fargone time's renewer, who
  can renew a goneby summer,
winter, or a wind that blew
            long, long ago.

Ah love, return my heart from dead
  and gone to wondrous hours,
give me golden times ahead,
let my heart and hope re-wed
  here among new-verdant bowers,
let their lovely vows be said
            as breezes blow.

NOSTALGIC SONG

O darling, on this summer day
    in Nineteen Hundred Two,
the parasol above your head,
    your shadowed eyes of blue,

the way your yellow hair is piled,
    the color on your lips,
the way you look at me and smile
    and touch my fingertips—

all these conspire to make me dream
    that we might fall in love:
yet what a jealous fool I am
    when I touch your glove

and feel the prints upon that glove
    of those hands of his,
and taste the ashes of old love
    as we walk and kiss—

    O darling, were there others
        before Tom came along?
    O darling, have I brothers
        among the Coney throng?

    O darling, when we marry
        will you be true to me?
    O darling, let us hurry,
        let's hurry up and see!

AN ACROSTIC

for my wife, Patricia Schorb

Poe wrote a riddling good acrostic once.
  DAvies turned trick into a feeling tribute
BeTh could take pride in. Well, I'm not a dunce.
  You**R** servant, you will find, is a glib brute,
ma'am. *I* am able, any time I choose,
  to do a**C**rostics cleverer than theirs,
Presto! **It** is the nature of my muse,
  Patrici**A**—money as to millionaires.

Now here i**S** what to look for: scan the page—
  then, if you **C**an't see anything, try counting
inward, from **H**igh to low. Soon a presage
  of what is to c**O**me, love, will form, this mounting
as you proceed. **R**emember, it's a name.
Patricia Schor**B**? You *got* it! Here's to fame!

POETRY IN MOTION

It was disheartening when physics told us
the universe was alien, indifferent.
I'm glad it's changed its doubting tune back to
the music of the spheres, of sorts;
especially now that I again see you
walking in the garden as you used to do
long, long ago. You haven't changed a bit—
gripping your brocade with one small hand
and with the other feinting flowers at the bees.
I'd have thought that I'd gone mad before,
but no more since the famous physicist has said,
upon accepting his Nobel, "It's poetry,
out there, and deep in here," pointing at his head.
"The microscope and telescope look in and out
but not across the warp and woof of time."
And that's where you go walking in the garden
(the garden of the old house that is gone,
the garden that's a parking lot downtown),
feinting at the bees with your hand of flowers
and lifting your brocaded summer gown.

TODAY, NOON TRAFFIC CROWDING

Today, noon traffic crowding, heat appalling,
I saw the double of someone I knew.
A face from long ago, I heard it calling
as plain as I might now be hearing you.

Thank God I'm not a king, or Canon Law
would have me married to the woman yet!
Pathetic creature! Not the one I saw.
That woman looked like one I would forget.

I mustn't be unkind! Resentment speaks.
So many years to hold a useless grudge!
Life's like a faulty sink from which love leaks.
Would you believe I stopped and couldn't budge?

    Forgive my grief, then, when I turn aside.
    I have at heart what I had thought had died.

RIVAL SLEEP

I have a rival for my darling's heart,
that dog called Sleep. She cannot let him lie.
It is the same now as it was to start:
she loves Sleep better than she loves my sigh,
my upright passion—which will never quit—
my tenderness of touch—all naked me!
She loves Sleep more than thunder's lightning wit
or downpour's sonorous profundity.

She loves Sleep better even than my kisses,
and cuddles him, not me, the long night through.
When I sat next to them and heard his hisses,
snake-tongued, in her sweet breath, I sadly knew
    that deepest Sleep would keep her in the end—
    my loving never could make her attend.

TORCH SONG

Lucky that you love me!
Lucky that you care!
Thought you'd treat me roughly
if I were to try
to attract your eye,
so I didn't dare.

Then one day you saw me
sulking in the corner.
No one came to paw me.
No one even tried!
Guess they thought I'd died!
Only you, a mourner,

staring at me there
with a solemn look
on a face so fair
I near fell apart
pounding with my heart.
Half the ballroom shook!

You came over then,
smiling, saying Hello,
different from other men,
smarter, I thought, somehow,
making your slight bow,
voice so soft and mellow.

Later, asking you
how it was you married
—I was feeling blue—
plain and simple me,
music ceased, and we
talked the while we tarried

on the muffled floor
waiting for the band to

play our song once more.
This is what you said:
"Dearest, your sweet head,
filled with bunk they hand you

—utterly unreal
books and films and such—
having the ideal
constantly in mind,
searching, will not find
answers overmuch.

Love has many reasons,
being what it is:
many different seasons
drifting in and out,
flowering in doubt,
freezing in a kiss. . ."

You fell silent then,
but the music rolled!
I felt gay again,
happy with alarm
dancing against the storm
which your words foretold!

AD ASTRA

A student of the stars stepped out one night
and scoped the glittering carousels of space,
the pinwheels whirling at colossal height,
and, lovely intricacies of midnight lace,
a train, from an amazing wedding gown,
with pale and gleaming bonnet (called the moon),
that spread above the tallest tree in town,
and saw where she had flown, much too soon,
deserting him when, with a wistful sigh,
fell at his feet those flowers never thrown.
Now like the stars she diamonded the sky,
as once her image starred within his mind,
and, finally, he saw how she had grown
beyond his scope, that he must cap and blind.

THE VANTAGE POINT

If you allow your thoughts to run, gray man,
utrammelled grist, along the belt of mind,
do you discover there one grain of truth,
or one remembered woman not mundane?
Was every step ill-chosen or ill-timed?
Your passion in abeyance, or patience rushed?

I stand at noon, and wonder at the night.
From where I stand the morning was of dun.
The afternoon ahead could be still worse.
I hope somehow to see it light and bright;
I hope somehow to share it with someone,—
a woman in my arms, both warm and wise.

FOR UNITY

Forster cried *Connect.*
Is there no way to correct
this unbearable condition
of lack of inter-recognition,
to commune, to sympathize,
even then to empathize,
to be on a path together
in the same weather
with a beloved other,
wife, child, mother,
or must miscalculation
of depression or elation
cause constant misconnection,
and be the sad projection
until the very end,
and all joys unfriend?
Hope, be harbinger,
not pretender, not stranger.
Love, let us be gifted,
by communion granted.

THE WIDOWER

    The clock of the cock at morningrise,
  or machine of the city sweeper,
rips the tape of the night from the wound of the day,
  painful to the sleeper

    who, hurled from his world of dreaming, hugs
  the airy shape of his wife
who left him most malignantly
  alone with his widower's life.

    Then, as his arms pass through the space
  that his wife has left in passing
and collapse within the O of prayer
  as if the man were massing,

    his eyes in surprise are opened to see
  that his prayer is sensual,
or that his prayer is a wife of air
  as the moon is menstrual.

    Thus, winning beginning again and again,
  though something each morning is lost,
he's gifted with pain to go on again
  by the wrinkled sheet of a ghost.

THE NORTH OF LOVE

I

Winter, that great doomed ermine,
challenges the serpent and the mouse,
buries each in his crude house,
silences the summer din
of birds: and bells ring across white silence
—where thickets are ungainly ghosts,
leaning together, gossiping in wind
—to herald a distant sleigh,
their chiming voices thinned
by the crystal distances of air
and the vast inertia of the trackless snow.

Through lacework windows
I see the bare white birch,
frail virgin of the timberline,
new bride of snow, the Eskimo;
I watch as he caresses
her modest, proffered limbs
and pale, gripping feet—
this mating of tree and snow
reminds me of all love . . .

II

When the phantasmagorial leafless trees blossom anew
    with blue, frozen tears,
and the wind-whipped snow at evening and the creeping
    mist make an indivisible ectoplasmic figure
that hovers above the lake and lurks near its frigid
    banks,
and the ominous cold evening sky describes the vale
    of lost things, with its gray upon gray of cloud
    upon sky,

and the moon is a pale disk in the pale, tall light
    of evening,
and the wind halloos down from the mountain like the
    voice of the Cyclops demanding more wine,

  and blindly it tumbles the house to one side;

when the dull, small stars go shivering about in the
    heavens,
and the serpent and mouse and the beaver and mole lay
    locked in their crude, white houses, afraid,

then we suffer from reminiscences of all the folly of
    the misspent years;
for winter is an end; above all a time of summing up:
    to take in hand and stop the spinning whirligig,
        your
life, to examine in the cold light how love fools,
    outflanks
you, takes you and makes you and breaks you again, no
    matter what sweet cynicism you think you have
        achieved. Do not try
to riddle this phenomenon any more than the heavening
hawk riddles his hunger. But remember the bare
    white birch, frail virgin of the timberline,

  the firnificated kisses of her bride-

groom gathering in cold, pallid clumps along her limbs,
    covens
of wind weighing against her, mountain-bred, bitter,
    flaying, as all love's too often made . . . .

III

I strengthen in this northern solitude:

When constellations wrangle overhead

71

and wind roars, the sudden shiftings cancel
the sound I listen for, the sound of bells,
and I fall into winter stupor, dreaming—
I dream of trekking up the mountainside,
the moon ahead, old-woman faced; behind,
the frail white birch, deflowered bride of snow.
I dream myself withstanding wind and cold;
and, breathing hard against the altitude,
of climbing up Love's Everest, to breathe
the cold significant wind of mountaintops.

FOR PATRICIA

A fleece of fine doves
is too crude,
Patricia.

A fleece of fine doves,
murdered for love,
is not enough.

III. LIGHT ~

LATE NIGHT RAP OF SOUL AND BODY

When you speak, and fingers snap,
it's I who tell you what to rap.
I own your hands, I own your feet,
I own all your dancing meat.

You have no home but meat and bone.
You are not you in space, alone.
If my bones break, you cannot move.
How then, my Soul, do you show love?

I'd shake you till the last bulb blew
and with the dawn do something new.
Your Soul, who's master of his ship,
says bell your sails from toe to hip!

You'd have me break and die for fair
from endless wear and terrible tear.
But no, I'll sleep. What can you do?
If I am tired, then so are you,

and when I sleep, you too must sleep,
and in your universe must keep,
among your dreams, inside my head,
a restful quiet in our bed,

till we awaken, straight and narrow,
freshened, like a new-fletched arrow.

DITTY

I

Valleys rich and beautiful
  make you wish to farm them.
Women wise and wonderful
  make you wish to charm them.

II

Once an innocent of loves,
  now a veteran of them,
I remove my velvet gloves
  to, barehanded, love them.

WHEEL OF FORTUNE

On Wheel of Fortune, Sex, to lick its chops,
sends Vanna's highheeled little feet across the stage.
    She wiggles, turning cards. My old aunt thinks:
"I never looked like that, even at that age!"
    And so it goes, as Vonnegut has said; and, like the Wheel,
we turn and turn and wait—for what we wait,
    we wonder. Maybe the Jackpot Prize,
the house we always wanted, and, at its gate,

    a swanky Maserati! The Wheel clicks
and rolls and clicks. We count to ten.
    My old aunt saves her dough (but we say bread—
or maybe not). Click click! My old aunt thinks: "Well, then,
    where to?" And in the glitz of Vanna's Fortune Wheel
time stops. The nervous neon blinks with doubt:
    click click, and click click click, and here
we are! The universe turned inside out

    and, young and beautiful, or handsome male,
eating each other up, we drool, O hungry for the flesh.
    Who's who? Who's where? Again: the spinning Wheel,
the flashing lights, Vanna's target fanny, and fresh
    turnings of a card! O laugh, O laugh and laugh!
O scream! Once rated the most popular
    program on Earth, the Wheel of Fortune
itself comes back and back and back, bright star!

THE STEROID LADY

The steroid lady stands, flashing her smile,
   upon a pedestal at Muscle Beach.
She's come a long way, baby; the last mile
   was not beyond her iron-willed, wiry reach.

Delts, lats, pecs, abs, obliques, gluts, hamstrings, triceps,
   erectus spinus: she walks in beauty like
a knight in well-oiled armor, flexing biceps,
   and spreading lats and giving traps a hike.

What hope for man is left? She's made of iron!
   She looks like Mike, my hirsute little friend,
but that she's hairless. Is she also barren?
   For mothers must have fat or hormones end.

The softness of a woman has been taken.
I feel as if my manhood's been forsaken.

THE FASHION SHOW

The slim young women float their subtle curves
   before a fashion-conscious audience.
Diaphanous enough to tickle nerves,
   their gowns lift off them in a breezy dance
as left leg forward forces right hip out,
   and small breasts, bra-less, bounce beneath a gauze
of punctuated pink. Their red lips pout.
   Their veteran eyes, dark shadowed, seek applause.

Young women and some not so truly young,
   whose art it is to show another's art,
can you be sirens of whom Homer sung,
   can so much softness be so hard at heart,
that you would make this hard-pressed buyer sin,
forget the gowns, and buy the mannequin?

THE BEVERAGE FOUNTAIN IN THE GYM

She urinated into tall-stemmed glasses.
Oh how they loved it, piss of pure champagne,
the golden bubbly! She herself was ice,
a frigid lady. It was then that bane
of sex, the matron's matron, passed the door
that thumped with laughter, looked, and saw *her* there,
who leaned back like a most provocative whore,
legs open, peeing, as if without a care,
her face carved into lechery; so the good
wives sued the school for sexual harassment,
and one divorced her husband, who had wooed
a work of art to her embarrassment,
    had wooed a lady of extreme bad taste,
    who melted in the heat of hate—sad waste!

BLARNEY STONED

Ah, Dionysis, ya grapey divil deity,
ya'd like ta have me back in Hellas
to guzzle in the juice of yer depravity!
Ya know yer dirty bottled blood'll
keep me at yer bidden.
Ah puke it up and force it down lak cud,
but I'll tell ya straight, ya satyr goat,
tomorrow, ah swear, ah'm quitten!
Ya make me drink this soupy slop,
ah know ya do, ah know it!
Ya tease me on ta gulp the rot,
and sure'n hell ah show it.
But ya'll not beat me, goaty beast,
cuz ah tell ya straight, ya satyr goat,
tomorrow, ah swear, ah'm quitten!

COCKTAILS FOR TWO?

John Ciardi
liked Bacardi
but drank Chianti
with his Auntie.

CAESAR AND CLEOPATRA

When Cleopatra rolled out from the rug,
it was the end of the Republic. Caesar,
involved in mid-life crisis, felt the tug
of pagan godhood, plus the need to squeeze her.
She took him on a tour of Egypt, showed
him secrets, like the tunnels used by priests
in their predictions of the Nile, and rowed
him on her barge. She showed him that her breasts
were fully formed, those of a goddess waiting
for him to join her in the Royal Way.
"A balding man should wear a crown." Her baiting,
her teasing, proved Great Caesar's feet were clay.
She laughed to see democracy go down,
and Caesar turn from great man into clown.

THE FINE ART OF HAUNTING

I

"Watch how," my teacher said, "when I tug, she tugs
right back, annoyed. She thinks she's caught on something,
then wonders, when she sees that nothing's there,
how she got caught—on what, on where? And now
she's baffled, for there's nothing near her sleeve,
no furniture nearby, no hooking chair.

II

And now she speaks to him. I think he's here, she says.
He thinks she's suffering guilt—There's no one here.
He pours champagne. She pulls her glass away.
She tells him that she feels your presence in the room.
Don't ruin the occasion, he tells her.
We've got his house and all his money and each other.

III

Yes, haunting is an art," my teacher said.
"You mustn't be too obvious, too crude.
They'll think it's all a trick, or caused
by natural tremors, earthquakes and the like,
and what you want above all other things
is to be certain that they know it's you."

ECLOGUE

Non nostrum inter vos tantas componere lites.
—-Vergil, Eclogues

FIRST SHEPHERD:

We meet again upon this hill
but now we climb it with a will,
when only last time, when we met,
our breath was easier to get.

I see your flock has grown greatly
over what you had just lately.
Oh, you'll die rich, but what's it matter?
Will wings of faith make your mound flatter?

SECOND SHEPHERD:

My soul is tended by a priest
whose duty it is to see to the least
among his flock as it is ours
to see to our sheep during their short hours.

FS: Much as you'd see to your fine flock
piece by piece on the butcher's block.
SS: We have had this argument before.
FS: Ho! Then, my friend, I'll say no more.
SS: Why do you plague me with dark thoughts?
You ought to think—
FS: Ought me no oughts
because you're a serious man who hurries
from hill to hill, enjoying worries
that do not matter, and I'm a herder
who knows how to laugh in the face of murder,
for what would the murderer be taking
and what would the victim be foresaking?
SS: You were a foolish fellow when
we last met, and are again.
FS: As indeed are you, who think you see

your way out in a fantasy,
in buying a pass to the eternal
from a priest whose heart's an infernal
machine of greed and mumbo-jumbo.
Did he have you drink his magic gumbo?
SS: Of dragon-bones. How did you know?
FS: I know many shepherds who go
to these purveyors of clipped toenails
and what you will. The game never fails
to take them in more than they do meat.
SS: I'm sensible.
FS: But they defeat
good sense because they offer what
good sense just simply hasn't got—
essence of Self, the thing we love,
outside, beyond the body, and above
that body's gross and greedy needs
which cause so many dirty deeds.
Your health is good. You need not worry.
SS: I do not worry.
FS: You heave and hurry,
and with your staff you vault the hill
as if to leap to heaven. Will
nor wealth can keep you whole.
SS: And when they tug and pull and toll
the bell for you, where will you go?
FS: What can we see? What can we know?
Go nowhere and become the sand,
a stuff run through the little hand
of an infant on a wide wide shore.
Like you, my friend, I'll be no more.
SS: Unbeliever!
FS: Self-deceiver!
SS: Your little flock is moving on.
FS: And I shall follow and be gone.
SS: Farewell, poor doubting soul!
FS: Farewell, and keep you whole!
    SS: Next year, perhaps—upon this hill.
    FS: If flesh is quick and has a will.

87

INDIAN ODYSSEY

In Memory of Acee Blue Eagle

I was afraid of the Indian boys
with no feathers in their hair
when I was twelve, in Oklahoma,
and went to school there.

They came at me, angry, red,
because I was from the East.
I did not know I should be dead.
I did not know I was a beast.

I tried to make them like me.
"See, this is my Red Ryder rifle.
Shoot it, shoot it, if you please."
They hurt me with that windy trifle.

Oklahoma is no place
unless you are Blue Eagle, Ace.

EDUCATION

Stemmata quid faciunt?
—*Juvenal*

Because he never went to college,
my father sold the Book of Knowledge.
Myself, I never went to school,
but did devote myself to pool.
Both of us ended on the rocks,
graduates of old Hard Knocks,
alums of Loving Kindness, yet
ignorant on how to get
along in life without degrees,
no forests for us, only trees,
yet publishing our poetry
in *Yale* and *Southern* and *Sewannee*.
Sometimes the editors write back,
Dear Professor, you're no hack,
we wish to publish "Ode on Birds"
in which we find such lovely words.
And I write back and say to them
I'm no professor, all the same.
I never even went to college,
but daddy sold the Book of Knowledge,
and I read it, growing up,
when he and I would share a cup
of sherry over Heraclitus
knowing nothing'd ever right us,
knowing nothing quite stands still,
that only changing always will
keep you up with changing things,
like that river on time's wings
that you can't step into twice
even if you'd pay the price.

Now that dear old daddy's gone,
I think I'll write about a swan.

OUT-PATIENT

I think about myself too much,
my hypochondria is showing.
I'm always sick with such-and-such,
I'm always glad my blood is flowing.

What's wrong with me I know too well:
I lack the necessary leaven—
my heart has skill to conjure hell
and my head is out of touch with heaven.

YEATSIAN SORROW

When Algernon Swinburne died,
most poets doffed their hats,
but Yeats leaped up and cried:
"Now I am King of the Cats!"

THE SQUID

Now let me tell you what he did,
this heavy-headed, squirty squid:
he tried to give his wife a kiss
and swallowed his domestic bliss.

A PhD?

That's Pig-headed Dope
according to Hope
in The Road to Utope.

AGENT SONNET

for Alex Jackinson

"Why don't you write a novel, for God's sake,
  get down to something good to read, instead
of solipsistic verse? Give us a break!
  Write something worth a read at night in bed.

The public likes a song, a song in rhyme,
  not free-verse pouting about the poet's life
in chopped-up prose, a reader's waste of time!
  The reader wants a story full of strife!

The reader likes a good detective story,
or else a horror story, good and gory.
  The public likes a bit of gruesome fun.

The public wants some sex; to be a voyeur;
to let a woman be a man-destroyer
  while islanded romantically in sun."

SYMBOLS

Pro Deo, contra ecclesia   Fidei Corticula Crux

1. THE CROSS

These Crosses are quite various in kind:
the ones the Romans punished with were wood,
but others have been precious metals, shined
by priests with polish, symbolizing good.
There's one which, on its side, looks like an X,
and symbolizes Scotland's Saint Andrew.
Another stays the vampire with its hex,
though many think that simply can't be true.

The Cross Impotens, with its crutch-like ends,
stands for St. Philip and St. Anthony—
yes, both, disabled, share a single Cross,
but, being saints, I doubt if either minds.
The Greek is lengthened, centered equally.
I think it mostly symbolizes loss.

2. THE FISH

What symbolizes baptizing in water?
An anagram in Greek, ichthus, or fish,
for Jesous Christos, Theou Uios Soter,
or Jesus Christ, the son of God, our Saviour.
When seen in Christian settings, make a wish
to have a happy life in which to live
(which Torquemadas never can forgive,
so don't let church spies notice your behaviour).

St. Peter was a fisherman, they say,
and one day caught a sole and then another
and soon his bobbing boat was full of fish.

All soles, he said, are one another's brother
(most women were excluded in his day),
and, rinsing it with wine, he cleaned his dish.

3. THE LION

The Lion's an emblem of Jerome, the hermit,
used to denote his death, and deaths of others
as martyrs in the Roman amphitheatre.
Nero did not have any need of permit
to throw these Christians to the lions. Mothers
would wail while watching in loud keening plaints,
but some would not let drop one little tear
for certain knowledge that their sons were saints.

It was a joyful day for them, to see
the lion's tooth transfix transfiguration.
Caligula and Nero were not gods
but did His work without their knowledge. He
made instruments of them, against all odds.
Death is God's mode of reinvigoration.

4. THE PEACOCK

The Peacock stands for immortality.
"The spirit passes from this life to more
and better life to come," supposedly.
The impress of the moment on the mind
may be as much as one will ever find
of depth and length in life and space and time,
and so much then for all fatality.
We may have seen the best life has in store.

The Peahen waits the Peacock's grand display
(she nearly always finds that it's enough
his immortality has come her way).
Perhaps the reason's in the thousand eyes

93

that like a strange horizon hypnotize
and egg her always on to call his bluff.

5. *THE DOVE*

The Dove denotes the purity of woman,
whatever that can mean beyond her love.
Well, I suppose it's something far above
what I can think of when I think as human,
and not as someone supernatural,
my mind an impure thing, half-animal,
incapable of knowing purity,
but not, I hasten, without sympathy.

The Dove is symbol of the Holy Spirit
and also of all females saintly dead.
I wonder how it is that we inherit
through Patriarchs unmerciful, rock-hard,
this image of unwomanly white love,
seeing instead of woman, bird—a Dove!

6. *THE DRAGON*

The Dragon stands for evil, sin, or Satan,
denoting how we fell before we stood
on our hind legs inside that scarey wood
that we remember now as Garden Eden,
a paradise and snakepit all at once;
and conquest over paganism, too,
as when "St. George the dreadful dragon slew,"
as when he proved that dragon was a dunce.

(St. Michael, too, was made extremely tense
by legless serpents and their fiery kin.)
Once, snakes were at the water for a drink,
as if the mild oasis were their sink

and not the desert paradise of men,
when stones of primates taught them better sense.

7. *THE LAMB*

Begin with sacrifice: an offering
made by all races, usually in youth;
made by the pagans as they groped for truth;
made by the primitive; a proffering
of something that we have for what we want;
almost of Isaac by good Abraham,
whose homeopathic magic was quite blunt;
also by Aztecs till the Spanish came.

Would Christ approve of such insanity
more than he would approve the rack or rod?
But publicists must make their stories tall,
and Saul it was, who, turning into Paul,
made sacrifice of Christ, the "Lamb of God,"
the centerpiece of Christianity.

THOUGHTS FOR LATER

No matter how clean we are, or how neat,
we always have dirt on the soles of our feet.
There's always the stuff in the cup of the tooth
giving to infancy, childhood, and youth
the pain and the poignancy which we forget
when we look back in time as if at the set
of a play which then seems paradisal and pure,
from the vantage of age and the pain that is sure.

COST OF FREEDOM

The Vanderhorns own most of Arkanstate,
the Heebeejeebeezes own Kent;
a few score others own the rest of Freedom,
and we, the people, pay the rent.

THE MORAL OF FRANKENSTEIN

The instauration of a revenant
can prove very unpleasanant.

WHAT'S THE MATTER?

Luv, as our particles impact,
    and bounce, as they needs must,
it should be clear, my dear, we are
    but dust disturbing dust.

LIFE SURPRISED ME;
OR, BURROWING MOLES

I only feared a little bit
that I might fail to make the grade,
for my Professor Gnome had made
the grade with even lesser wit.

At first, I wanted for a theme,
like Yeats, then thought a campus idyll
(which Brits pronounce to rhyme with fiddle)
might be the thing to make my name.

"Publish or Perish," terrorized me,
so I worked late into the night,
and to my wife I would recite
my work in progress, "Life Surprised Me."

But then I thought too bold a title
might seem insensitive to some.
It must not shock, but seem to hum
(inaudibly at a recital).

"Burrowing Moles" seemed better to me
than "Life Surprised Me," loud and brutal.
My epic work must gently tootle,
or its strong echo might undo me.

Because the heart is like a mole
that pads about beneath one's feet:
It has a pitter-patter beat,
but is quiescent on the whole.

CABIN-FEVER BLUES

for Rodney Formon

Rain, rain, rain for forty days & nights—
  rain & more rain, dark rain days & nights!
But I can still remember bright white lights.

Rain, rain for forty days & not a beam,
  no, not a beaming smile of light! Jim Beam
keeps me afloat in all this flood, I deem,

Jim Beam, branch-water, music, memories,
  branch-water, music, memories, & sighs.
Outside the door the drenched cat cries & cries.

All dark outside the room & dark inside—
  It's so damned dark you'd think that I could hide,
& darkness is a thing that can abide!

I'll bring the cat inside out of the rain,
I'll bring him in to share my blues, my pain.

THE SOLD PIANO BLUES

Sold the piano,
I sold the piano,
   sold it to the husband of a blind soprano,
because I needed money
so I could pay the rent—
I needed money
so I could pay the rent—
   they had to make their living,
   I had to pay my rent.
(kept my guitar)
Sold that piano,
I sold that piano,
   the gap-toothed one that wobbled on three legs,
my poor piano,
   that made that sad soft sound
like when you're breaking eggs,
one dead pedal,
   many missing keys,
   its ivories all yellow and its broken knees.
Sold my piano,
oh I sold my piano
   and now I have to do a cappello blues.
(No, I don't—kept my gitfiddle)

Got no piano,
I sold it
   because I needed money so I could pay the rent.
Sold my piano
   and now I wonder where all that dirty money went
because I didn't pay the rent.
   I bought a month's supply of booze
   and now I sit and sing *a cappello* blues,
a cappello blues.
Ah. . . I sing the sold piano blues.
(good thing I kept my geetar)
I sing the sold piano blues,
sold piano blues. . .

NOTICE TO MODERNS

You solipsistic sissies, male and female,
poets about the Me, Myself, and I,
should send yourselves, and then collect, your email,
and not pretend such jots are poetry.

"Poets are actors, and their books are theatres,"
wrote Wallace Stevens. Roethke spoke in tongues.
How many voices spoke through William Shakespeare's?
Create verse worthy of great scoptic lungs!

There is a gathering on a green hill
where scops will sing of everything they share.
In my imagination, with my will,
I try to see that time, and who was there.

Or in a book or on a stage I try
to tell of others, not Me, Myself, and I.

BALLADE OF PRIDE

They're a proud people.
—The Frugal Gourmet

Of every group whose food he shows,
    this Doctor of Diet, this Frugal Gourmet,
this chef whose goodness simply glows
    and who doesn't know there'll be hell to pay,
    we need not ask just what he'll say,
for he shouts it from the TV steeple
    like the old ham actor in the play
When the Master Race Meets the Chosen People.

He shouts of any group he knows,
    "A *proud* people, those from Cathay;
those, too, from Kilimanjaro's snows."
    He doesn't know there'll be hell to pay
    when these proud people meet someday.
I wish all this pride would go and sleep ill.
    But meantime let me get out of the way
When the Master Race meets the Chosen People.

Proud Capulets, proud Montagues,
    proud Hatfields and real McCoys all day,
proud people everywhere, God knows,
    and who doesn't know there'll be hell to pay?
    They make you want to kneel and pray
that you needn't hear another peep till
    ugly young pride is old and gray
When the Master Race meets the Chosen People.

When Evil meets Good, as it will on the way,
who wouldn't know there'd be hell to pay?
Heaven's buried beneath a deep hill
When the Master Race meets the Chosen People!

101

SONNET AT SIXTY-FIVE

Sixty-five orbits of the sun today
and, though I'm growing tired of this spacesuit,
which rag, as an unhappy by-the-way,
has lost its goggles and at least one boot,
so that I cannot see or even walk
as I once could, and have some trouble hearing,
and toothless too, and tongue-tied, cannot talk
without the noise of cranky broken gearing—

where was I?—tired of this spacesuit!—still I
am grateful that I have a suit to wear
at sixty-five, and wouldn't I be silly
if I preferred to lie in earth bone-bare
   to orbiting the sun again this year
    in this old-fashioned and bedraggled gear?

CANDY BUTCHER

fragments from an unfinished musical

Characters
Jimmy, a candy butcher
Elliot, Jimmy's father
Fay, Jimmy's mother
Kosmo, Brandy & Stoney, candy butchers
Singer
Flame O'Hair, a stripper

Scenes
Minksy's Burlesque Theatre
The Midway Hotel

Scene: Theatre
PROLOGUE

JIMMY
(*rembering shining shoes of Lola Albright,
the movie star*)

Kneeling upon your
knees on the ground
kneeling upon your
knees and around
you the city
making its noise
shaking with pity
for shoeshine boys
who were not kneeling
as if in a prayer
who were not dreaming
of lost summer fields
and sweet summer air
always were scheming

103

and fighting for places
always were stealing
your hard-won spaces
and beating you up
and beating you down
all over town

and then to have seen her
all bright like a star
at night to have seen her
as if from afar
as if you were off
in some summer field
all alone with the night
when suddenly light
caught your eye
and you looked up to see
what it was in the sky
that was shining
all bright!

*   *   *

CHORUS

Nobody's blue,
it's Nineteen Fifty-two.
Come with me, Mike,
I'm voting for Ike.
It's odd or even, son,
so maybe Stevenson.
But nobody's blue
in Nineteen Hundred
Fifty-two!

*   *   *

SINGER

The most beautiful girls in the world
are at Minsky's
oh, they're dandy
oh, they're handy
oh, Minsky girls
are the most beautiful girls
in the world!

(candy butchers enter)

STONEY

Ice cream, orange drink
and gurly magazines!
Eat, drink, be merry,
see the pictures of the Queens!

KOSMO

Tom, Dick, and Harry
have an orange drink!
Ice cream, orange drink!
Gurly magazines!

BRANDY

Got a changer on my belt.
Buy before my ice creams melt
from the pictures of the Queens
in my gurly magazines!

KOSMO

Buy my pissy orange drink

and stand and sip and stop and think
of what the show was all about
then you'll never leave without
the pictures of the Queens
in my gurly magazines!

ALL

Eat, drink, be merry
Tom, Dick, and Harry!
Buy the pictures of the Queens
in our gurly magazines!

*   *   *

FLAME O'HAIR
(appears in Jimmy's dream)

I'm not what I seem to you.
I'm just a dream to you
because you're so young.

You're what you are to me,
a boy very far from me,
because you're so young.

When I was your age
I dreamed of a prince—
I haven't dreamed very much since.

(speaks softly)
When you are my age
you won't dream of this Flame,
you'll dream of me young.

(singing, fading from sight)
I'm not what I seem to you.
I'm just a dream to you

106

because you're so young.

*　*　*

Scene:　The Midway Hotel
DUET: THE BICKERSONG

ELLIOT

I'm in a lovely state of grace.
Indeed, a happy paradise—
my robe, my Chesterfields, this place,
my glass of sherry filled with ice—

Don't send me to the desk below,
down to the mundane world you prize.
There's much of wisdom you don't know.
Believe me, this is paradise.

FAY

This is a dump
and you're a lump
of a drunk
on a trunk!

Calling me a peasant
is not a very pleasant
thing for you to do,
even if it's true.

Your father was a rambler
after women, and a gambler
who lost your mother's farm
and brought you all to harm.

Had he any virtue,

how could he so have hurt you?
Why, we'd be rich today
if your mother'd had her way.

But this is up to date!
At the awful awful rate
you are going, we are going
on the sidewalk when it's snowing

and the wind is blowing!
They are going, going, going,
without the slightest doubt,
they are going, going, going
TO THROW US OUT!

*   *   *

SONG: THE GAME OF LIFE
   Elliot, Fay and Jimmy

ELLIOT: See if you can make it in the world out there.
It only has the meaning that you give it.
See if you can make it in the world out there,
Make it a game and live it!
What's the difference in the end if you win or lose,
Dead if you do and dead if you don't?
What's the difference in the end if you win or lose,
Either you will or you won't?
There's nothing in the world to say you're wrong or right.
You got to make it up as you go along.
There's nothing in the world to say you're wrong or right.
In the gamble with life you've got to be strong.
You've got to be brave for a while at least,
especially when you're young.
Got to be brave for a while at least,
at least till your song is sung.
Now I'm an old man so I really don't care,
and I sit around here and I think.
Now I'm an old man so I really don't care,

except for another drink!
I had you so late that I'm no example,
for a young uprising son—
I had you so late that I'm no example—
FAY: No example for anyone!
ELLIOT: See if you can make it in the world out there!
JIMMY: (*chimes in*) I'll see if I can make it in the world
    out there.
It only has the meaning that I give it.
I'll see if I can make it in the world out there,
make it a game and live it!
ELLIOT: What's the difference in the end if you win or
    lose,
dead if you do and dead if you don't?
JIMMY: What's the difference in the end if I win or lose,
in the end, I will or I won't!
ELLIOT: There's nothing in the world to say you're right
    or wrong!
JIMMY: I've got to make it up as I go along!
There's nothing in the world to say I'm right or wrong.
ELLIOT: In the gamble with life you've got to be strong.
JIMMY: I've got to be brave for a while at least,
Especially when I'm young!
ELLIOT AND *JIMMY:* Got to be brave for a while at
    least,
At least till our song is sung!
FAY: I'd like to make it in the world out there.
It only has the meaning that you give it.
I'd like to make it in the world out there—
make it a game and live it!
In the gamble with life you've got to be strong,
You've got to be brave for a while at least.
In the gamble with life you've got to be strong,
At least till you've sung your song.
Now you're an old man and you really don't care,
and you sit around here and you think.
You're an old man and you really don't care,
except for another drink!
But I'm a woman who's still quite young,

109

just a wee bit past my prime—
you've got to understand that I'm still quite young
and I'd like to use my time.
I'd like to have a castle a chateau or a house.
I'd like to have at least a quiet flat.
I'd like not to run a hotel or rooming house,
or anything at all like that.
I'd like to pay our rent right out of pocket,
and have some furniture that's really ours,
and not to be afraid that you would hock it,
and to sit and dream for months and days and hours.
Yes, I'm a woman who's still quite young—
ELLIOT: But you married an older man.
FAY: But I'm a woman who is still quite young,
and I'd like to do what I can.
FAY AND *JIMMY*: Let's see if we can make it in the
    world out there.
It only has the meaning that we give it.
Let's see if we can make it in the world out there,
make it a game and live it!
ELLIOT: Now I'm an old man so I really don't care.
JIMMY: I'd like to be somebody in the world out there.
ALL: You've got to be brave for a while at least,
especially when you're young!
Got to be brave for while at least,
at least till your song is sung!

Curtain: End

IV. TROUBLE ~

THE BOSNIAN CHERRY

. . . the explosion appears to have
shocked the tree into blossom.
—Reuters

Friends, look with faithless unbelieving eyes
upon this miracle the bomb has wrought,
as now, in shocked conversion, I tell you
of spring against the devastated skies
of winter war, the hopelessness war brought,
and how, enveloped in explosive blue
of acrid smoke, this tree could still devise
beyond predictability. It caught
the shell's enormous heat, and grew
fluid with sap, miraculous with surprise
of spring, for all combatants to be taught
anew a faith unlearned by deathly cries,
a blossoming the human heart has sought
with every hopeful spring—a sweet-peace prize.

PEACE IN OUR TIME

O yet we trust that somehow good
Will be the final goal of ill . . .
                                    —*Tennyson*

The poet, ignorant philosopher,
Alpha & Omega beggar, posits
AND, in an academic naming, the
world that takes all others in:

"AND," he says, "includes the All.
OR is us & even war.
AND will keep including more.
OR is reductive, what we recall

—particulars, parts, & particles
—how many ways can it be said?—
all things unborn, & all things dead,
commas, grapes, seeds, articles

of various sorts, & written ones,
all things that are not All,
all memories we can recall,
all less than All, all suns,

all galaxies, germs, & viruses,
all parts of atoms & their parts,
all stops, reverses, starts,
all flowers, roses, irises—"

She frowned. "And so you say," she said,
"that you can live with ugly war
because it's what you call an OR.
ORs also are the many dead!"

"Yes. When struck by this, I wondered
what horrid meaning it must have.

114

The morality of love
was made to seem almost a blunder.

And yet, I thought, morality
must include the act of war.
For Fascists must be fought, are OR,
are fragments of eternity

gone wrong in AND, the All; are Fear.
A kinder & a gentler love
has got to be beyond, above,
& other than, this OR-world, where

it must be that, if we could see
the whole of things, we'd understand
how piece by piece (& hand in hand)
things add to form in synergy

a greater than is each alone,
as also are twinned Space & Time,
or life in clay & death in lime.
Thus, in the AND, all Ors atone."

DARK AGES

More light!
—Goethe, on his deathbed

Oh, there was never any powerful light
by which to comprehend the common day,
merely the milktoast light of the benight-
ed, who cannot understand what we see.
But whose fault is that if we sadly try,
standing clumsily up to our full height
like doomed, dim-minded begging bears
that with sad clumsy hearts are so unbright?

Is it any wonder that all we do is fight?
Is it any wonder that all we do is lie?
Is it any wonder that what we write is trite?
Is it any wonder that we stand and sigh,
   who are graced with only such a little sun
   by which to try to be someone, anyone?

THE LEAP

Faith says to leap, forget the brain;
  Brain, I am Without-which-not.
Many a night I have lain
  in my bed and, cold and hot
by turns, have tossed,
and known the cost

of ambiguity about
  which way to go: if I should throw
away the brain, be like some lout
  bulldozing what I do not know,
without clear sense
or evidence;

or, on the other hand, should pray
  that I can make the leap of faith
and throw the troubled brain away,
  and so acquire at my due death,
through sacrifice,
a paradise.

HOT TEEN HOGS

They rub the blue out of their bluejeaned crotches.
  They rip the teeth out of their red-hot zippers.
  They fan the flames, and then curl up like kippers.
At last they check their charioteering watches.

They tell each other where to meet next week.
  They shake their leather jackets free of gunk,
  and she with red nails combs her ducktailed hunk,
as he wipes damp mascara from her cheek.

From this day forth their dream becomes to make love
  naked in bed, not fake it in a park
  behind some bushes in the evening dark.

They swear that not again will they forsake love
  in greasy leather garments, harshly studded,
  to go home dirty, lying, and guilt-flooded.

BOXER BALLAD

for Moe Schwartz

A lightweight in those days,
  now he's a heavyweight
(the booze, the cheesecake, stays).
  At age twenty-eight
things were looking good,
and he did what he should.

But Beauty was a lady
  out to be a star—
contender, a little shady—
  determined to go far.
She might have made it, too,
had life been kind and true.

A gangster was the gent,
  out to steal his love,
a man who was hellbent
  to be so much above
all others that he fell
finally to hell.

They never got fame's joys.
  He had to lay him out.
That gangster and his boys
  cost him his title bout
and she did not get far
toward that Broadway Star.

A chorus girl, a gent—
  it's people happen, son.
It was his main event,
  the last one that he won.
For wrong things came out right.
Love won his toughest fight!

119

42nd ST., 70s

When I've gone out to walk at night,
to tour the streets, mean-dark, false-bright,
of this sick city that is no home
but for the Giant and the Gnome,
the Monsters of Despair, I've seen
pathetic sights, and sights obscene:
  The fat black man who has no eyes
but two great holes from which he cries
long hours, holding out his cup
for Times Square crowds to fill it up,
while eyes of Dog who stands beside,
show that *his* soul has surely died;
  the legless men who crabwise creep
on wooden gloves to morning sleep;
  the woman with the bleeding leg
who climbs the subway stairs to beg;
  the varicosed, tumescent, sick,
already dead and yet still quick;
  male hustlers, leaning in long rows,
posed in mock movie-hero pose;
  porn shops with tainted men inside
some of whom have kissed a bride;
  retarded vendors at their stands
masturbating, hiding hands
beneath big stacks of filthy mags;
  and drunks on jags, and hags in rags,
asleep in doorways commandeered
from rats and stiffs; the other weird
displaying signs of coming doom
Hellfire and Brimstone in the tomb;
  and faces stupified by dope,
expressionless of love or hope—
  these sights and worse are near Times Square
at night when I go walking there.

THE MANWOLF

Among the wolves a tale is told
of how, when Moon is full,
some normal-seeming wolf becomes
a Manwolf, stalking, murdering all.

His fangs grow short and flat in front,
his paws grow long and fingered.
He holds a firestick in a hand,
makes fire with what is called a trigger.

The cubs who listen to the tale
howl in fear of such a fright
as wolf that looks like human horror,
naked, murdering day and night.

SUNDAY QUESTION

Now Sabbath bells are ringing happiness
for saints without the need. But what of us,
the still unrisen sinners of the sun
who run through grassy woods towards our ruin?
We, the innocents to wisdom; the birds, the beasts;
we who, famished, kill, and then who feast;
we the deaf the dumb the blind the hurt and hunted;
for us the tale of Sabbath bells is blunted.
Come and explain, O understanding saint;
we wish to worship, even in complaint.

THE MORAL

Some say the world will end in fire . . .
—Robert Frost

My father died in fire.
My mother dies of ice.
Myself? It is desire.
So ruinous a price
we pay for what we need!
The Muenster needs of mice
have trapped them in their greed.
It's never very nice.

My father felt the mire,
and threw decisive dice.
He died upon a pyre
with roomers and with lice.
A churchman of the creed
succumbed to shoes and rice,
then found he couldn't breed.
It's never very nice.

My mother feels with ire
the lack of kind advice,
and will time really buy her
another paradise?
A mongoose met a weed
and bit him off a slice,
then started in to bleed.
It's never very nice.

Myself, I'd be a liar
to say I have no vice.
I'll do it till I tire,
I've said so once or twice.
A hound who took no heed
once tried to make a splice.
The lion had a feed.

It's never very nice.

So all of you who read,
for you let this suffice:
that we shall be agreed,
it's never very nice.

DIRGE FOR THE DEAD STUDENTS
(Kent State University, Ohio, 1970)

She'd only come to look
when bullets broke her flesh
A frosh, she held a book
  when bullets broke her flesh
  with almost wistful sighs
  Her face was round and fresh
With almost wistful sighs
the bullets raped her body
with almost wistful sighs
  they pierced her gentle body
  and her book dropped open to
  a page all torn and bloody
her book dropped open to
a torn and bloody page
containing nothing new
  a torn and bloody page
  each child must learn to read
  a "History of Our Age"
each child must learn to read
O study, students, study
this "History of Greed"
  O study, students, study
  learn what they want from you
  another age as bloody
is what they want from you
another age befouled
and nothing else will do
  another age befouled
  by Great-Granddaddy's Greed
  (no wonder Ginsberg Howled!)
O Great-Granddaddy's Greed
sucks, like a Vampire Bat,
the blood of his living seed
  sucks, like a Vampire Bat
  the blood of our youth away
  sucks, like a cornered rat,

the Pestilence of Our Day
and spits into our faces
the horrors of Our Day
  and spits into our faces
  spreading disease and death
  that virus among the races
spreading disease and death
destruction throughout the world
with its maddening murderous breath
  destruction throughout the world
  that Malthusian explanation
  Picture the bombs being hurled
that Malthusian explanation
and a baby crying for shelter
while the Senate is on vacation
  and a baby crying for shelter
  and her mother and father dead
  and the bombs dropping helter-skelter
and her mother and father dead
and the President making decisions
(who will his daughter wed?)
  and the President making decisions
  Search and Destroy is the way
  and the President making revisions
destroy all their crops on the way
and the baby is blown to pieces
while the President goes to pray
  and the baby is blown to pieces
  while the President speaks to God
  and the rich collect rent on their leases
while the President speaks to God
and the students are shot for complaining
and the Haves of the world think it odd
  that the students (who Have) are complaining
  (these children have so much to learn!)
  and the government's busy explaining
for these children have so much to learn
in double-talk tripled twice over
how we keep what we get when we earn

in double-talk tripled twice over
how Ends do all Means justify
in News-Speak all wrapped up in clover
how Ends do all Means justify
and death to the man who denies it
so, hush up, dear students, or die!
  For death comes to him who denies it
  as many dead children could tell
  and praise to the bastard who buys it
as many dead children could tell
and four dead students provided
a proof in the sun when they fell
  these four dead students provided
  us all with a living example
  that day in the sun when they tried it
gave us proof and a living example
of what the "Great" in their greed are about
and four dead students are ample
  to show what the State is about
  (Christ, any one baby who died
  should have left us no shadow of doubt!)
Now four young students have died
shot dead in the name of the law
(but in fact for the lies they denied)
  SHOT DEAD IN THE NAME OF THE LAW
  FOR THE TERRIBLE TRUTH THAT THEY SAW.

MURDERER'S DAY

Why is it always Murderer's Day?
Why can't it be different someday—tomorrow?
I wake to the sad and terrible news
and ask over coffee, "Why do I listen?
Why do I want to hear of the fire?
Why don't I turn from the morbid to music?"

Of all things on Earth I'm sure I love music
better than any—I could listen all day.
Is it fear that impels that the ghetto on fire
be the thing that I hear today and tomorrow,
though I ask over coffee why I should listen,
when I wake up, to such terrible news?

On goes the radio, blasting the news.
Why don't I tune in some beautiful music?
Why do I listen? Oh, why do I listen?
And why is it always Murderer's Day?
Why can't it be different someday—tomorrow?
Why is the ghetto always on fire?

Why is the world always on fire?
On goes the radio, blasting the news.
Why can't it be different someday—tomorrow?
Why can't the world be filled with sweet music?
Why is it always Murderer's Day?
So I ask over coffee, "Oh, why do I listen,

why, over coffee, do I sit and listen
to news of a world that's always on fire,
to the latest report of Murderer's Day?"
But on goes the radio, blasting the news
instead of some beautiful, good-morning music.
Why can't it be different someday—tomorrow?

Why can't it be different every tomorrow,
that never again over coffee we listen

to other than beautiful, good-morning music
describing how love is aflame and afire?
Why can't there be music instead of bad news
and no more reports about Murderer's Day?

Oh, don't let tomorrow be Murderer's Day!
Let there be music and no sign of fire,
and let us all listen to much better news!

WAR TWO WORDS

for Elbert Harkins

"There is a mounted gun on a flat-bed,
and it is firing at some splintered shed.
I hear those high-pitched screams that multiply—
a Kindergarten!—then a bullet sigh,
and something forms inside me like a node.
Life stands above me and recites the Ode
to Melancholy. I stare at the blue sky
and see it for the first time, and it's *God!*

Two purple hearts, two silver stars, and I
am home for a parade to glorify
my hero's part in that dark episode.
I understand the latest bombs *im*plode,
suck in and swallow, following my view
that monsters eat their children, *a la mode!*"

THE NIGHT SWEATS

By our intensity, with hanging head,
we spell the wolf away, who pants and croons
outside the door, who wants us to be dead
so he may have his meal. By magic runes
we rid the world of wide-winged evil loons
whose madness mixes metaphors instead
of bringing clarity, whose looney tunes
make breathless nightmares in our sweat-wet bed.
Hear them who creep toward our peace of mind,
destructive artifices of our brains,
to wreak their havoc! Run, leave them behind!
And in the dark we try to run in chains
and can't escape because the night is mined
to blow us up in spite of all our pains.

NIGHTWATCH

My loneliness was deep.
  I could not see beyond it.
It robbed me of my sleep.

I lay awake, saw sheep,
  counted; no dream responded.
My loneliness was deep.

The tide was at the neap.
  I took the moon, and donned it.
It robbed me of my sleep.

I heard a great bird leap,
  die, singing as the swan did.
My loneliness was deep.

You sow and you shall reap;
  for guilt was how I conned it.
It robbed me of my sleep.

"Lord, take my soul to keep!"
  I cried. Not He: no one did.
My loneliness was deep.
It robbed me of my sleep.

THE POWER GAME

The king is weak, the enemy has planned,
the queen is powerful and vain, and vain,
and everywhere there is a helping hand.

The enemy has landed on the land!
Who is afraid of fear? The pain! The pain!
The king is weak, the enemy has planned.

The pawns go forth and die. They understand
their queen is beautiful, not plain, not plain,
and everywhere there is a helping hand.

Her knights are paramours. They leap or stand
according to her will. The gain! The gain!
The king is weak, the enemy has planned.

The bishop says a prayer. The castle's spanned
by other drummers than the rain, the rain,
and everywhere there is a helping hand.

Yes, trouble plagues the kingdom. Undermanned
and understaffed, they try, and strain, and strain.
The king is weak, the enemy has planned,
and everywhere there is a helping hand.

AS GOOD AS IT GETS

I

Why does the Pope's tall rocket hat point up?
Because God's will has been removed from matter
so that we might decide what's right and wrong—
we, who are madder than the maddest hatter,
our every word a snippet of mad song;
who've served the heads of people on a platter,
or blood in a tureen for Sunday soup!

II

Karl Barth said we were no damned good. Yes, he
shared Jeffers' view of humankind. Karl Barth
was probably correct, if we agree
to measure by his standard. But what hearth
was ever won or kept by kindness? What we do,
if measured by that which we could do, seems
somehow to suit all but the elitist few.

SHADOW OVER AFRICA

I

The great black shape below us
is the shadow of our balloon.
A fair wind drives it, casting
a pall upon native loon
and hippopotamus—
but what if the dark is lasting?

II

The antelope leap at hearing
our wind chimes on the air.
Do they fear what we bring in our flight?
Do the deaf snakes hear?
"Humans are nearing, are nearing,
bringing their circle of night!"

ELEGY FOR THE LEADER BIRD

This compass-headed bird,
>dead-reckoning South in Fall,
arcing its bloody breast
>above the roof and cawing
some kind of bold farewell
>to higher air and leaderless
V'd fliers off on it,
>was shot (we saw and heard),
and staggered in the sky,
>dripping blood and guts
down on the lobstered roofers
>working in the sun.
It sang its downfall swan
>song silently, now, spread
its wings, and then, as silent
>as its eyes, it lay
resting on the roof,
>face up, and looked at clouds,
(and some sweet heaven we
>could almost see); but soon
pain shook it like an angry
>nurse, so one good roofer
struck head from body with
>a spade, merciful severance,
and catwalked off, bloody
>spade dragging on the tiles,
a man of dirty duty,
>unlike the murderer
of song, the wanton boy-
>in-man, who pellet-shot
the bird (the shot we heard);
>and this once musical,
most bright and beautiful,
>small dust was part of all.

KYRIE ELEISON

Tonight the house across the street is sunny
with flames. It crackles with a solar static.
It brightens night as if a star had landed.
Hardworking people like ourselves, we think,
but thank our lucky stars it isn't us.
Yet, What a world, we sigh but do not say,
and to propitiate the gods, like Greeks,
invite the poor souls in to spend the night.
Then stand and watch the final sparks fly upward.

The fire trucks take their slowly-clanging leave,
their tolled bells sounding in an exequy,
while my poor counterpart consoles himself
with certain clauses in his policy,
a standard H.O.P., but without flood;
for we are on high ground and need not brood
about the water-levels hereabouts
becoming a dramatic factor. Nor earthquakes.
This rock's been stable now for centuries.

REPORT THE DEAD

Not having been, the dead remember only,
or never, never having been. Remember?
Remember never, ever being lonely?
They smell no smoke from any dying ember,

or, forever never being, what is smoke?
The dead remember nothing very clearly.
Nothing is very clear, the silence spoke.
Forever is as loud as nothing, nearly,

but nothing is the loudest silence now,
and never, ever speaks of what it knows.
Report the dead for never knowing how
to entertain the living with dumb shows.

Report the dead for scaring us with Not,
the nothing, nothing, nothing that they've got.

BRIEF BALLAD

I live alone with my wife
who lives by herself with me.

Late sleeper, early riser,
big talker, shut-my-mouth,

our life together is apart;
apart, our life together.

We have no intimacy, we
have quality time together,

have quality time together.
Sure, no clue to each other,

and we've got to sleep apart,
in separate rooms, dreaming

not of each other, but no other,
of halls and doorways and walls.

Thirty years, how well
we know each other, how well

could be called not well at all,
thirty years not well at all.

Why do we stay together?
Because we have been together,

and no one knows us better,
no one knows us better.

THE SAFETY ZONE

Bald Samson, feminized and impotent,
king of no castle, least of all his own,
resides within the modern Safety Zone
in what he calls the Nest of Discontent.
Like that great monster of the Scottish loch,
he sometimes finds his head above the water
(his neck is of his body a full quarter)
and, bullet-bald, heads in toward the dock
that promises escape, but's tugged below
and back and down, and his head sinks from where
there is a full supply of fragrant air
to where air-breathers should not try to go,
to where at bottom lies Contention's Bone,
the Nest of Discontent, the Safety Zone.

GOOD WORKS ARE LOVE

Today I noticed, randomly,
on my shelf of poetry
Bill Empson and Bill Williams
sitting side by side,
the scholar and the doctor,
Seven Types of Ambiguity
and "No ideas but in things"
the intellectual and the
know-nothing natural man.

The war between what each
was representative of
is still alive, but why?
Each wrote poems one can—
admire? Each did his thing.

To think that in an art
requiring tolerance, at least,
a war abides between two ways
of working words for what they're worth
—it troubles, reminding us—
does it not?—of all intolerance,
of the religious wars, and of
the white-sheeted racist and
the hanging black-skinned man.

PUB SONG

The jukebox unwinds a Piaf
  to us as we sit at the bar
trying to find some relief
   from a world where troubles are.

The bartender brings me my drink
  and I drink it without a remark.
Outside, the evening is pink
   with that pink that comes before dark.

"I regret nothing," sings Piaf,
  and the record drops dead in its box.
Now Piaf is free of the grief
  her glorious music mocks.

And drunk, I am free as a sailor
  to bless or not to bless.
Say, how can a man be a failure
  if he has no need of success?

MARTIAL MUSIC AT A BAND CONCERT

Now, as we hum a rousing martial tune, a Sousa,
a "Marching to Pretoria," an "Over There,"
what we are doing is the conjuring of courage,
that necessary, difficult, quixotic friend
who'll leave us in a lurch but then return to save us,
who, like a hero, leads us on to take the hill,
to take the burning pillbox hill of day, and hold it
until the smoke is drifting off and evening falls.

We need this friend more than we do the light of reason.
So do not sing to me of love's romantic passions,
nor of fraternal fellowship, nor happiness,
but conjure with me in a rousing martial tune,
or march with me to some tin drum that brings it out,
that courage necessary to our daily lives.

HEART FAILURE

I have made my moon landing at night
by way of the emergency ward,
on the strong black arm of a nurse.
My wife is the other woman,
and between the two women I enter,
seeing, reflected in glass, my red car
half up on a curb, and mal-angled,
the glare of the high beams showing
my terrified wife's confusion.

There is no air in that car,
there is no air in the night,
but there is air in the hose that the nurse
claps to my turning-blue face,
and strength in her arms that are used to
the harsh struggles that have plagued her existence,
strength that I finally can share in.

I lie in a gown in a room,
and the silent killer says nothing.
He signalled, I guess, with red flags.
I paid no attention. I'd developed
an elephant's hide, an armor for the arrows
of insult that poor boys endure.
From childhood, when I was raw,
and my nerves could actually bleed,
I worked on this suit of armor,
oiled it and flexed it and shined it,

but now it belonged to them,
the doctors who probed me with wonder.
"Didn't you notice a thing?
You sound like a sidewinder, rattling."
"I thought I'd caught cold in the chest."
But I had no desire to know
because I had no desire to stop.
I could see that they thought, "What a fool!"

144

All but the black nurse, who knew
how the poor slid the slippery slope
that poverty, stress, and high blood pressure
grade for the struggling-upward.
She pulled at my ear, and said, "Tough guy!
He don't take no crap from his heart."
She knew how the pressure builds up,
as you climb in the ignorant ghetto,
until you would break, or be broken.

"How you doing, baby doll? Better?"
"Yes, but now I'm embarrassed."
—embarrassed at being so weak,
ashamed of my heart that can fail,
ashamed to have such a heart—
no lionheart, no Coreleone, I.
But they tell me it's stress that's at fault:
the heart is okay, the tests show.
The angel nurse flattens my hair,
pulls at my ear, and says, "Go!—"

SAPHICS: PRAYER WITH AD HOMINEMS

Grant me, America, continuing freedom from
those officious intermeddlers who would
save me from myself, busybody bores ever
      vigilant to steal

freedom from our land & our land from us for
spotted owls & kangeroo rats & snail-darters;
puritans without the old God; Pantheists,
      pagans of Gaea.

Dear, endangered country of mine, grant hope of
triumph, victory over leftwingers like
these officious intermeddlers, that I
      may not lose you to

them, whose empty lives must be lived through others,
whose *raison d'etre* seems to be control over
people, whose cowardice quivers at freedom,
      O my America!

THE APPLICANT

The day perfused its natural light, but here
the indirect fluorescent lighting gave
a ghastly look to marble walls and faces
and like a psychotomimetic agent, produced
its odd effect: she saw her life go by her
just as they say all drowning persons do.
Bright artificial light fell from the air
as she looked on, and strangers swam the lobby
as if they were a vague sea-life, dull clots,
and she among them like a thing in tide,
and all the while her life kept going by
as if the pages of a book were turned,
a morbid album scanned in lurid light.
She saw her early youthful face, and then
her latest face (but that was in the red
art-deco elevator's gilt-edged mirror)
and nearly missed her floor for concentration.
Then she was spoken to, and told her name,
poking her *New York Times* ahead of her
as if its roll of news contained a proof
enclosed within it, like a royal-cartouche,
and wiped the perspiration from her brow
and took an offered chair, and waited.
Suddenly her name hummed in the shell
of deep-sea office sounds her ear had pressed to
and she went forth to do as she was told,
but fuddled in a kind of difficulty
that her officious tester could not know,
and missed the bell (they rang the one bell only).
The lady gave assistance, tried to help,
betraying, nonetheless, suppressed impatience.
What sort of person are they sending us?
And yet she was amusing to the rhythm,
a nervous smiling creature, out of place;
a feckless angel fallen out of grace.

TRACT

The human race is richly blessed,
for it's at liberty to choose
the path above the dark forest

where it evolved from small tree shrews.
When we were young, in those dark ages
when trees were gods, we could refuse

our few objective pilgrimages
their bright discoveries forthwith.
We'd stronger gods and images

of potency surpassing truth.
It wasn't innocence we had
but ignorance, like any youth.

And ignorance of good and bad
we can't equate with innocence,
for ignorance is something sad

and innocence is happy; hence,
that Eden Garden written of
to show our disobedience

could not have been a place of love.
Nor did the ignorant within
(whose bodies fitted hand-in-glove)

deserve God's angriest chagrin
for plucking knowledge from the tree.
How was their action any sin
in seeking knowledge, lovingly?

ON MUDDLING THROUGH

I like the English saying "muddle through."
It's always better than perfecting things,
although the human race keeps trying to,
keeps carving for stone Victory stone wings.

V. FORCES ~

THREE BY HERACLITUS

I

Offend yourself with mirrored knowledge
(where's that face you wore at college?)
and your sense of life's no-stasis,
thinking of various times and places,
recalling the endless grandmother summers,
remembering bees and thunderboomers,
and quote, "A boy's will is the wind's will."
All is flux, nothing stands still.

II

About to vacation some years ago,
it was yourself that you wanted to know,
so you left your wife behind and went
away to the mountains and set up a tent,
and re-read Walton, and cast your fly
as you did as a boy, long and high;
but something went wrong—and you got a fever.
You can't step twice in the selfsame river.

III

Discontent in retirement you stare at your land
(once wild but tamed by the work of your hand).
How long will it take to overgrow
when you are gone, you'd like to know.
You haven't the strength to do things twice.
It's all gone now, gone in a trice.
You're an old dog now, a dog with the mange.
Nothing endures but change, change, change.

ELEGY FOR A LATE TORNADO

I

No, Nature has no wrath, no, none at all, and you
are merely what you are, Tornado—or by some
counts twenty—touching down around this tarheeled state,
a thunderbooming menace innocent as pie,
the product of two airs, of heat and cold colliding
without intention in our Mother's general chaos,
O fearsome Mother of us all, who says take that
and see if you can take it, kid, or you're not mine.

II

Now we of social order must adjust insurance
and see what can be done about the fallen roof;
and too, some trees have fallen and a boy is dead,
and we must bury him, the poor unlucky lad
who stood too close to leaves while saws were lopping limbs
for safety's sake; and others, too, who died in homes
turned round as if they rode a carousel or flew
like helicopters up, foundationless on Earth.

III

How do we call the dead back? Well, She says we don't.
She says She doesn't care if we are fools enough to live;
and what are houses but the homes of hermit crabs,
delectable to cats, fish and furry felines both;
and what are we to Her, She says, sure not the best,
but who dare say She doesn't love us all? Tornado,
you were a special pet of Hers a day or two,
but now your short-lived reign of terror I record.

IV

And you were dead and now are gone and none of us
can show a thing but that some still endure, survivors
in pain and struggle and somewhat the stronger now
than otherwise, and though a small reward for hurt
reward it is, and in the aspect of eternity
the very thing that shapes the human race, and all
the injured creatures of the planet as they struggle,
not merely struggle—stronger, propagate—O Winds!

TO THE MIND

The mind can take flight into the world,
because it is not purely of the world . . .
—Kenneth Patchen

Why do we wish upon a nonexistent star?
We know the star is gone, the light just now arriving.
Then why, O Mind, do we not wish upon the light?
Why do we lie both to ourselves and others, why
do we not value more the facts you would supply us
and make the bravest and most honest use of you,
you burning glory in the darkness of all time?

Why do we mock our truest selves and glorify
the sad bear of the body, locked in gravity,
O glorify the little leaps that it can make,
when you soar through the universe, a rocket ship,
you your own torch, and looking for the cosmic key
with which to unlock all existence in a phrase
or elegant equation, speaking like a god,

explaining everything in terms your partner, Heart,
retarded, slow, but pulsing, an idiot-savant,
can bear to beat his muscled drum for and be gay?
O Mind, you bravest human part, you essence us,
and lift us off our feet in flight toward the stars,
and are our pilot in the windshear night to port,
and so I sing your praises all my days, O Mind!

THE KITE

From the dark, tarred roof where urchins chant
in garbled language some insistent word,
the line leads upward to the bending rod,
spine of a skin that billows in the breeze:
the kite, a pterodactyl, hovers high
above the threatened eyes of three small boys.

There's little safety in the dangerous city,
the toys of children change into the ogres
of their bad dreams. Oh many times I've seen
a smudged dragon who had terrified his friends
stand screaming in his metamorphosis
until his mother's arms recalled his name.

So now: a phantom of pre-history
is hovering above the very roof
where these boys stand, eyes staring up in awe.
It shudders in the wind; the shining tail
of multi-colored terrors coils and snaps,
like tentacles of a drifting man-o'-war.

And as they watch, the afternoon drifts on,
diminishing the day, and evening falls,
until at last, yet suddenly, it's night,
and hunger wakes the hypnotized to time.
The boy who holds the line begins to haul
his monster from its perch among the stars.

Descending in the darkness, huge, aglow,
it seems to seek its prey among the three.
They watch bewitched, enchanted for a time,
a fascinating nightmare coming true;
but as its membrane shadows chimney stacks
and falls upon them, tenting out the view,

they cry aloud, and bolt toward the door,
one frozen hand still dragging the bad dream,

five others struggling for it to be free.
Then, at the door, they see the line slide up
suspended from the belly of a bat,
a giant bat whose little hands they see
attempt to tear their line—umbilical, their line.

RODIN, BALZAC, AND *THE THINKER*

Because assemblers will let us place atoms
in almost any reasonable arrangement . . .
they will let us build almost anything that
the laws of nature allow to exist.
          —K. Eric Drexler, *Engines of Creation*

Atomic transmigration was beyond Rodin,
who could not finally touch his statues into life.
And yet he must have seen the likeness of his art

to that of universal processes, stone into soul,
and felt the homeopathic nature of his magic,
the sympathetic magic of his mastered art.

But if Rodin could catch an atom in his hand,
then he could build a living man from solid rock,
then he could make him think and be a tender lover,

could make Balzac emerge from what was holding him
and step down from his pedestal and have a drink
and tell, as only Balzac could, where he had been,

of what the world of rock was like before the soul.
But once out of the rock, Balzac could never tell
Rodin about the rock, nor why his touch must fail;

and if Balzac could never tell, how could Rodin
make great Balzac march forward from the marble slab?
It must be that Rodin confronted his conundrum

and sat down like *The Thinker*, head in mighty hand,
and thus inspired himself to yet another task—
to show poor humankind its constant puzzlement.

ODE ON SEX

I

Come, let me champion your cause, mind-altering Sex,
disintegrator of great family names and fortunes,
despoiler of priests, wild joker in each Jack and Jill's
young life, who eggs their egos on aggressively;
delightful Sex, who makes us foolish to ourselves
in alleys or in cars or in motel rooms rented
in titillated glee and paid for all our lives.

II

Come, let me champion your cause, mind-altering Sex,
for Mother Nature gives no whit for social problems,
nor loves the individual more than the whole;
cares little for the personal life, or not at all,
but is a painted slut, big-bellied and prolific,
drugged drunk on hormones, sprawled with open legs and mouth,
and ignorant of consequence—"couldn't care less!"

III

Come, let me champion your cause, mind-altering Sex,
for whom in Tijuana town I paid two dollars cash
and two weeks on the isolation stool when I was young;
who bows and bends the gay and kills them for their trouble;
who loves no one but lusts for every orifice—
O Sex, mind-altering Sex, sad Sex, are you all bad?
O Sex, then what is Cupid's so sweet Psyche for?

IV

The juggling of the genes—the double-helix shuffle,
survival's muted laughing need to mix us up—
causes the countless changes in two families

160

in lines that branch back into great antiquity.
See them as weaving an enormous web shaped like
a geodesic dome, our primal mother-creature
at bottom and at top two families conjoining.

V

When Jack and Jill, the twins, the scared and hungry ones,
the little red, white, brown, or golden berries, come,
give them a shower, sharing wealth and love alike,
for Sex brings Love into the world with motherhood,
and even orphans know the heart above their head
that shook the womb they grew in, know another there,
and know most certainly the need, mind-altering Sex.

ON AN INLAND ISLAND

off Pamlico Sound

On this calm coast the small iambic waves
  remind me of Shakespearean blank verse
  that some apprentice actor must rehearse
repeatedly, as echoes speak in caves.

It almost makes one fancy life behaves—
  because it's hard to think of something worse
  than this salt zephyr, unequipped to curse,
while watching here, where palms are calm as graves.

  And yet they tell me that the hurricane
sent tentacles of wind and water here,
while wreaking havoc off on far Cape Fear,
  and that a storm-surge drowned the chatelaine
whose hideaway stood near this very beach,
which one would think was simply out of reach.

THE PRAYER

I

Today, the hurricane is coming.
Many are already dead, floods
rise like megalomaniacal hopes,
birds have been stolen by wind,
broken, or beaten off into peace.

II

My umbrella broke off, spinning away
in the wind like a whirling mushroom.
I was left with the hook in my hand
and a face like a Keystone comic.
I boarded the bus to applause.

III

The hanging signs flapped wildly
and one, like an ace of spades,
was dealt to a wagging dog.
A shopkeeper recovered the corpse
while the bus hummed in horror to go.

IV

"It could have been me," an old lady said.
"The government does us no good!
Oh Lord, stop the wind in its
irreverent rush, stop the rain,
stop all that we cannot control!"

NOW, THE FOX!

A thousand times I've had this urban dream and
asked a doctor what it meant
  to no avail. "It was the city's grip on
an impressionable child,"
  one doctor told me. I was dropped once down a
hellish, pitch-black pit, a deep
  dumbwaiter shaft, and fell a floor before I
landed, more or less intact.
  I bear a scar above my eye. Could that be
it, dropped by a drunken man,
  a family friend, when I was still an infant?
Meaning harmlessly to play,
  he swore off drink, I'm told. In any case I
have these nightmares constantly,
  and doubt if they will ever go away. Waking,
after one, I'm shaken to
  the bone. I live now in the country, where I
hoped to find diminishment
  of terror, over time. But here's the strange part:
rabies is a major threat
  here in the country in the summer—dogs and
cats can get it from the wild-
  life teeming in the woods—and just the other
night I dreamed a foaming fox
  that chased me back into the cityscape I
hoped so much to free myself
  from, years before, by coming to the country.
Waking horror brought me new
  concern for peace of mind and where to find it.

DREAMSCAPES

I

Now go the seven wreaths of weeks:
sleep slips out like a moon-sucked sea.
The heaven-high haggard hero-rogue,
the cygnet, circles and he sinks
beyond the grindstone and the spur,
baptizing waters with bird-brogue.

II

Now go the garlands and the grave
down Time's counterclockwise lake
where good and evil are one law;
nor the lusty wives of leapyear rave,
but plumb the depths by plummet, wake,
and breathe the rose's claw.

CRUEL GAMES

I

I read somewhere about a wizard with computers,
a man who's made a myriad millions in the field,
who lives out in an island's perfect solitude
in order best to think about life's origins,
who seriously thinks our universe is bits
and bytes, a program made some cosmic Otherwhere.

II

We make computer games ourselves and love to play them,
why then might we not be a game for something else,
a smarter It, why might it not be true that we,
the world, the universe, are toys played in an Else,
a game called Life, or its equivalent in Else,
played by the happy children of the clever Its?

III

Truly the Demon of Intelligence must thrive
among the happy Its of Else in Otherwhere,
but one must notice all the cruelty of the game
and think that those in Else have not evolved as yet
to that high point that even we, their bits and bytes,
their pawns, aspire to daily in our average lives.

IV

I must look up that article about the wizard
and find his name and write to him and ask him how
he thinks the whole thing works, and if the software used
is durable enough to keep us going on until
our progress takes us well beyond the happy Its
of Else in Otherwhere, who play such cruel games.

THE WAR OF THE NINE AND THE SIX

Jane Goodall tells of the Nine and the Six,
the Chimps' War,
of how a tribe of fifteen male chimps
divided, Nine and Six,
and made new camps.

The Nine, she writes, because stronger
numerically, attacked
the Six, several to one,
isolating, murdering each of them,
until there were none.

These had been sons and fathers,
friends and brothers,
but had become two nations,
sniffing at borders—
foreign relations.

FORTY ACRES AND A MULE

Thoughts while sowing

Just when your hope is highest for the vow
  of Time to be your friend and earn the deed,
it droughts your spring and breaks your brand-new plow.

Is this the way that Time will do us now?
  Time most betrays you when you're most in need.
Just when your hope is highest for the vow

of Time to golden calve your finest cow,
  she and her calf both die of poison weed.
Time droughts your spring and breaks your brand-new plow.

The weather always wins, no matter how—
  too hot, too cold, too wet, too dry; indeed,
just when your hope is highest for Time's vow.

Does Time protect you from the butting prow
  of sun-dried wind that skims topsoil and seed?
It droughts your spring and breaks your brand-new plow!

Foreclosure looms ahead, the hanging bough
  of an old lynching tree. Should you concede,
just when your hope is highest for Time's vow?
Time droughts your spring and breaks your brand-new plow!

THE WHITE STALLION

It seems there is a place
where beggars and poor people go to tell tales,
and the mostly riding moon will park to look
and to listen in the dark to the tales as they are told
  by the poor beggar bards of the hobo jungle,

a place lonely as life,
at the end of the track, in a cul-de-sac
of starred, campfired night, in a turntabled copse
in the dark ragged green of smoke-stunted oak and rope-strong
  weeds, where birds bivouac: and of all beggar bards

who sang a sad ballad
there, for the folk, or chanted a moon-watched tale,
the most famous because most magical was
the hobo bard the Pinkertons called "The All-Seeing Eye,"
  because of his blind, superhuman vigilance,

and the mooncalf folk called
"O'Shay the Irish Shaman" for his gift of
curative power, uncanny control
of events, and for divining the deep, hooded meaning
  of things beyond their poor eyes and plain powers to see.

Now O'Shay rose up and
loomed before them, above them, his flame-mapped face
red and changing as the cat-o'-nine-tailed fire,
his great, blind eyes like those of the horse of his inner-eye
  (a carp-eyed stallion), his hair a red, swimming flame

dowsed by the cool waters
of the moon. O'Shay, though blind, was free, though poor,
was proud, and did not like to see the poor folk
bowed by that boulder, Care, nor bullied by the railroad dicks
  and afraid in their camp at the end of the track

169

underneath the parked moon
in the starred, turntabled copse where he loomed now,
watching their weak eyes with his strong, inner one,
and knowing that they needed a hopeful tale to be told
    that the Depression be lifted, courage restored,

            and the parked moon set free
to ride the night into dawn, and new hope for them,
crying: "Pride's the subject of my moon-watched tale.
Now listen to O'Shay, poor people, and see what you think—
    stop, look, and listen with the fascinated moon.

            "There was a white stallion
that lived when you were but babes of scuttlebutt
at heaven's height; nay, that moon itself unborn
of the great, swaying sea; a stallion of clouds and spirit
    that came finally to gallop the great plains of

            "the North American
west; a pale, proud, bellows-nostrilled, carp-eyed king
of a horse, that could blow back the floozy wind
from Manitoba down to the plains of old Mexico;
    that could whinney across the west to call a brood

            "mare from her happy home
to him a thousand miles away in the night;
that spoke in trumpeting tongues of his freedom,
stamped, and neighed pride from his great, rampant heart; who
    hammered hope
        with his hooves to the ranging mustangs of the plain.

            "A maverick king, he!
And this is the best part, for the horse was blind
like myself, and nothing daunted, unconstrained,
for he saw with his four, steamed, cow-catcher hooves, and his
    ears
        that could hear the baby-breath sigh of a willow

170

"on an unborn wind; saw,
too, and best, with an inner eye like my own,
and had powers, like myself, gifts of nature,
with which he could divine the treachery of humankind,
    and thus keep himself free, and wear no man's hot brand.

    "For he wore no man's brand;
and that was a heartache to all rich ranchers
who had heard of the white stallion: his freedom
mocked their staked, barbed wire; and they offered gold for his
    capture—
    pots of rainbow gold those rich ranchers offered the

    "buck who captured the horse;
gold, gold beyond a poor cowpoke's wildest dreams—
fifty thousand dollars in gold bullion to
the buckaroo who brought in the phantom of the prairies,
    fifty more to the bronco buster who broke him—

    "fifty thousand in gold,
one hundred thousand in gold bars to do both!
They came from the stretched limbs of the continent—
wranglers, roustabouts, beggars and poor people like ourselves,
    all with mad schemes to capture the blind, white stallion,

    "keen on the trace of gold."
Here O'Shay's brick jaws mortised, his lips ringed teeth,
and his dark sockets fixed face after face, saw!
And yet they knew O'Shay was a blind man and could not see
    the mad excitement that they felt, hearing of gold,

    could not see how they stood
who had sprawled or hunkered down on their heels here,
could not know, therefore, how ready for pursuit
they were, how each in his mind saw a fleece-white phantom flee
    his grasp, as O'Shay took pause from his moon-watched
      tale,

171

and they cried out to him
suddenly, as one many-voiced, to go on.
"Mad men with mad schemes!" cried O'Shay. "For they knew,
the earthly fame of the phantom being, by now, widespread,
     that all the ordinary methods of capture

     "had been tried and had failed.
No, a ghost must be caught in some other way.
Hence these mad or tragic traps. One loon dreamed of
speeding hoopsnakes that would ensnarl the steed's cow-catcher
   hooves,
     another's gold-frenzy fancied a fast balloon.

     "The supernatural
horse and the idea of gold had made them mad.
Not all, some had sounder brains and better schemes.
A wrangler, a strong man who knew his horses, had staked out
     an arroyo which was the haunt of the white steed.

     "He pitched camp and waited;
and happenstance his patience was rewarded
when, like a mirage, the pale, maverick king,
with his own remuda of mares prancing and curvetting
     behind, galloped up to drink, stamping and snorting.

     "The wrangler climbed a rise,
and, twirling an Indian-charmed lariat
of rawhide interwoven with shot-gold wire
which he had bought from a Kiowa shaman, roped him,
     looping the golden noose neatly around his neck.

     "The white stallion whinnied,
rose rampant, and snapped the charmed, magic lasso
as the wrangler might have snapped a golden thread;
and the still-noosed stallion and his mares vanished in white dust.
     But this was the closest that any man had come."

     O'Shay stopped his story
here, drank from his flask, wiped his mouth up his sleeve,

and looked intently out at the poor people,
who had begun to suspect that he was not blind at all,
  so seeing seemed his ragged, flame-valanced sockets.

      And now they felt that he
could see them fingering their necks, golden-noosed
now, like that of the horse of his long, tall tale;
fingering their necks and feeling the golden noose tighten
  as they pulled from the shaman, and snap, freeing them.

      Suddenly O'Shay laughed,
and the rubbernecking, neckrubbing folk shook:
but then there seemed to have been no laughter there
but merely the bark of dogwood flame from the heeling fire
  or the sudden gold caw of a blackbird, bivouacked

      nearby. O'Shay frowned, now
and said: "Having heard how the wrangler had failed,
the rich ranchers upped the purse to a million;
but before any could claim it, he must represent them,
  having won a competition for horsemanship

      "from among the finest
cowhands and vaqueros to be found; and then,
having conquered all men, must conquer the horse.
The competition involved every truck or skill of
  wrangling science and art, and lasted a twelvemonth.

      "A vaquero triumphed,
and had fine mounts stationed at mile intervals
from a wheel's hub out for a hundred hot miles,
the hub the arroyo where the horse had escaped the noose,
  the fine mounts the posed spokes of a great wagon wheel.

      "The vaquero waited
at the hub of the wheel for the phantom horse
until it appeared, and the pursuit was on
for a hundred miles, mile on hot mile, with fresh, mile-new
  mounts,

173

for the vaquero hoped to exhaust the phantom.

          "But the great vaquero
could not exhaust or overtake the white steed,
who taunted him with his easygoing gait;
and, after his hundredth horse had dropped, could only report
          that the golden noose still hung from the phantom's neck.

          "News of the hunt's failure
spread up and down the plains, told by range riders
on lonely duty tours, at starred, campfired night,
until word reached a famed trapper up in Manitoba,
          one who had trapped every kind of animal.

          "His name was Hawkeye Red."
O'Shay paused here to take a swig from his flask and
to consider the beggars and poor people,
who were amused by the blarney of their shamrock shaman,
          who again managed to relate himself to

          the pacing white stallion.
A few friendly hoots were heard, with which, O'Shay,
scrunching a flame-snake of brow in a dark wink,
returned to his tall, romantic tale. "Hawkeye Red," he said,
          "left his cold northern home and journeyed far southwest

          "to find the white phantom,
or to find out where he might be found. Then he
methodically began work on his great trap.
He gathered the strongest oaken lumber that could be found
          and built a great stable in the arroyo where

          "the horse was golden-noosed,
and in it placed the most beautiful young mare
that the rich ranchers possessed among them, a
doe-eyed, blazed-faced bay with black mane and tail. Ringbolt-
     tethered,
          high-strung, frightened, Bonny-Pru would be the bait.

"Now he set the trap doors,
cleverly contrived to clap shut behind the
white horse when, or if, he entered, trapping him.
After making sure that the trap would work, Hawkeye
Red and the rich ranchers went to a vantage point

"to wait for the phantom.
Under the riding moon, Bonny-Pru pulled, kicked
the oaken planks, and whinnied for her freedom
across the dappled night, until her fearful, fearsome cries
were borne as on an unborn wind to the white steed.

"The man-watched moon rode high
as the hours passed and nearer and nearer he
galloped with all his magical might toward
her in her trap, and his; but at last he came to the dark
and looming stable; and, though the great, mouthing
doors

"gaped open, paused, galloped
away, circling wide the foreboding building;
then, though he knew this was a trap, galloped in
to the distressed, stable-trapped, ringbolt-tethered damsel mare
who cried out for a brave champion like himself.

"The trap doors shut! Silence.
No sound whatever from inside the stable.
The rich ranchers whooped high for their victory;
but, somehow, Hawkeye Red, now rich, felt saddened by success.
All left their vantage point and approached the stable.

"But, nearing it, the doors
split, splintered like kicked glass, spilled, filled the spiked air,
and up and over the heads of Hawkeye Red
and the rich ranchers rose the white steed and his damsel mare
like two wide-winged, magical, legendary birds.

"Hawkeye Red shook his head
in unbelief, turned, dazed, to see them, bullets

that followed the riflings of infinity.
In a moment of wild, unholy desperation, he
     ran to his horse, reached for his rifle, aimed and fired.

          "The rifle exploded,
but from the breech, not the muzzle, blinding him.
And in that first blind instant he saw the horse
of his mad pride go free, the white phantom rise rampant and
     neigh,
          like a musical muscle that flexes and sings,

          "and vanish from the land,
with his blazed-faced bride, Bonny-Pru, by his side,
never to return again." The poor people
were on their feet, now, whinnying, and galloping in place,
          for O'Shay had turned them into happy horses

          who would wear no man's brand,
who applauded their pleasure with hoof-clap hands
and tongues that rode the roofs of moon-watched mouths.
"Hawkeye Red," he said, "regained his vision, but saw no more
          with his outer eyes but with a strong, inner one,

          "and lived to tell the tale
at the end of a track, in a cul-de-sac
of starred, campfired night, in a turntabled copse
in the dark, ragged green of smoke-stunted oak and rope-strong
          weeds, where birds bivouac." And he set the moon free.

THE BIG CRUNCH

Upgathering, the dead are born again,
the dirt unshovels and the coffins rise
into the hands of backward walking men,
relieved, rejuvenating pallbearers.

A widow is again a married woman,
a wife, the mother of such lovely children,
these crying adults crying now like infants.
A hearse drives backward down a melting road.

From funeral parlor back to hospital
the warming body of her husband goes
by backward racing ambulance and crew,
who desperately try to save his death,

and watch in horror as his chest reopens,
and hear him laughing heartlessly at them.
They are too young to save him now and cry
at their own helplessness and nippled need.

Young, powerful again, he forges back
into the marketplace where he was born.
His girlish wife has lost her backward children,
forgotten them, but hopes to have some soon.

The objects of his life come rushing by;
his stature changes; and his wife is gone;
he vanishes inside his mother's womb.
The cemetery turns into a wood.

The world becomes a gas and joins the sun,
the sun becomes a part of many suns,
and suddenly the stars collect and vanish,
and everything is one again, just one.

THE DIFFICULTIES OF EPHEMERA

I know that the difficulties, as harsh as they are, and they are,
are, if not the purpose, the pastime of space, time, and star,
and what we are in is a vast starry game never to learn,
where all of the stars, like our lives, are only to burn,

and nothing's sacred in particle pool (or ridiculous quanta-
    flux),
and ultimately the planet's unsaveable—but, stop!—not because
    of us,
but because it's an observable rule of ephemeral existence
that ephemeral existence has only a temporary persistence.

And yet all of our consciousness-time we hold a wild power
to do as we think that we may for an instant or hour,
to move a few pieces or particles this way or that
with our particle claws and particle jaws of a Cheshire Cat.

FROM BROOKLYN HEIGHTS ONE MORNING

When, in the morning remnant of the moon,
the restless city stirs beneath the stars,
its buildings hunching in a black tableau
that forms Prometheus from common themes
of steel and glass and brick, I walk abroad—
for an hour now—while night lays claim on time
for the first time for me tonight (and now
already it surrenders to the sun!)—
I walk abroad requiring only love;
that it may be a morning gift unwrapt
from this dark shapeless parcel and received
in utter nakedness; that it be light!
But more than having light, I want to be
one for whom light adventures into change,
and gives me place to say in certain praise:
O Light, allow me several such days!

KINDRED SPIRITS

I

The kindred dead have taught me how to sing.
They hover in the wind at night, I say,
and chant in dirges while they're hovering
in readiness to hold my breath away.
I've heard the dead elm's charry branches bend
under the weight of Nobody-at-all,
until a greater ruggedness would rend,
were it desirable to them, and fall.

II

I know they're in my mind—they tell me so—
down deep within the labyrinthine lobes;
they dance and whistle in the wind, I know,
somewhere inside the gray and outer robes.
But they project themselves into my yard
and frolic like the children of their past,
obscene and awful, shrunken up and charred,
that I may see their funeral at last.

III

They fall upon my sleep and, when awake,
they mock me underneath the midnight moon.
They say that I am drowning in the lake,
they tell me I will strangle on a spoon.
I can't so much as take a simple bath
without the water rising to the rim
and looking at me with a look of death,
as though to say, This is the end of him!

IV

What have I done to them? Why torment me?
I know the inner laughter they must feel.
I've seen that bird, reflected in the sea,
that made the Mariner go mad, until
he troubled purity with his sad tale
and dragged the wedding guest down with the dead.
I do not know if I shall rise or fall
or live as something different instead.

METAPHYSICS OF THE BIG WOMAN

The Big Woman is sweeping the floor.
There is dust in the corners, dust
in motes in light at the door
and whirling along the walls.

It has been twenty-four hours
since last she swept the dust;
but, to the dust, being small, it is more,
by some counts, ten billion years.

Quickly, she bends with a rag
and wipes a world from the world:
for all of the dust is shining,
radiant, with light from her source.

UPSTATE STORM

Heavenward, at middle-height,
where the moon is cumbersome,
like a pale breast on the sky,
hanging big, and full of seas,

clouds coagulate, then darken,
curdle, into angry gray;
shed appendages adrift
in the rising, warning wind.

Thus they hover, sheep, above,
turned about by barks of wind
as the baa-waymenting lambs
can be turned about the field

by the windy barks of Dog.
Bent electric lances snap
(violence claps the whirling air),
blasting black a mangled oak

(cedars cinder at a stroke);
thunder echoes over hills,
rolling in the wind beyond
tangled and uprooted trees;

pitchforks fill the lofts with light;
carp-eyed horses leap away;
flooding rivers jump their banks,
drowning lowland cattle, sheep;

and the farm foundation quakes
with the force of wind and rain,
heedless of the life it holds;
cold, indifferent to pain.

REFLECTIONS IN A DOUBTFUL I

Is the peripatetic part of the meaningless goo
this autumn that is being trounced by the rain,
one with the fallen beaten leaves? Camus
and Sartre would insist on seizing pain

by the throat and giving it a throttle,
being that we are all alone with it
like a drunk in a rented room with a bottle
and not a 'toon in which to spit.

Up to us, they would say, to do something about it,
be a "Renegade" or find *No Exit*
or become one's own kind of Mister Fix-it,
but of its ultimate use, I doubt it,

doubt we can do it alone,
doubt it to the bone.

GOODBYE TO MYSELF

Goodbye, myself, whom I have loved so well,
   when you are not around me, I'm alone,
  but then there's not a me to be around,
alas, not even one for heaven or hell,
   unless you count a carcass, broken bone
  under a sunken lid under a mound,
or ashes in a box, or in a breeze,
   instead of slow decay beneath the ground.
   Goodbye, myself, without you I shan't groan
but be my bravest, like those lonely trees
  that fall without a sound.

ABOUT THE AUTHOR

E.M. Schorb is a prize-winning poet, novelist, and short story writer. As a poet, his *Murderer's Day* was awarded the Verna Emery Poetry Prize and published by Purdue University Press; and his collection, *Time and Fevers*, was the recipient of the Writer's Digest International Self-Published Award for Poetry and also an Eric Hoffer Award. Other works include *50 Poems*, Hill House New York, *Reflections in a Doubtful I*, White Violet Press, *The Journey and Related Poems*, Aldrich Press, *The Ideologues and Other Retrospective Poems*, Aldrich Press, and *The Poor Boy*, Dragon's Teeth Press, Living Poets Series. The title poem, "The Poor Boy," was awarded the International Keats Poetry Prize by London Literary Editions, Ltd., judged by Howard Sergeant. Schorb's novel, *Paradise Square*, received the Grand Prize for Fiction from the International eBook Award Foundation at the Frankfurt Book Fair. *A Portable Chaos* was the First Prize Winner of the Eric Hoffer Award for Fiction. But Schorb maintains that he is first and foremost a poet, and his poetry has appeared in hundreds of publications, here and abroad.